FINDING YOUR PATH TO PUBLICATION

A STEP-BY-STEP GUIDE

JUDY PENZ SHELUK

Superior Shores Press

PRAISE FOR FINDING YOUR PATH TO PUBLICATION

"Based on experience and extensive research, Judy has created a digestible and easy-to-follow guide for anyone diving into a new world (to them) of publishing. Sometimes it's hard to think of your creative masterpiece as "a product." Judy's guidance both respects your creative process and at the same time presents the realities of the outside world after the writing is done.— K.D. SULLIVAN, AUTHOR OF *A CURE FOR THE COMMON WORD* AND CO-FOUNDER, UNTREED READS PUBLISHING

"If you have ever wanted to write and publish a book, but didn't know where to start, *Finding Your Path to Publication* is for you. Built on years of experience as a successful author and publisher, Judy Penz Sheluk lays out the steps to getting your book out into the world in a simple to follow format—everything from making sure your book is the best it can be, to branding and social marketing, to pitching your baby to potential publishers. If you are new to the world of publishing, this in an excellent guide to making your dreams become a reality."—MIKE MARTIN, CO-FOUNDER, WRITERS FIRST

"A comprehensive resource for anyone interested in the business side of writing and the latest publishing options. Chock full of practical tips and sage advice, Penz Sheluk delivers the information in easily understandable bites with an insider's knowledge. A highly recommended must-read for writers at any stage in their career."—BRENDA CHAPMAN, AUTHOR OF THE HUNTER AND TATE MYSTERIES

Finding *Your* Path to Publication: A Step-by-Step Guide

Copyright © Judy Penz Sheluk 2023

Research Assistance by Emily Nakeff

Edited by Emily Nakeff and Ti Locke

Proofread by Nicky Hill

Cover art by Hunter Martin

Published by Superior Shores Press

ISBN Trade Paperback: 978-1-989495-54-4

ISBN Hardcover: 978-1-989495-55-1

ISBN e-book: 978-1-989495-56-8

ISBN Large Print: 978-1-989495-57-5

CONTENTS

THE WRITE LIFE

ADDITIONAL RESOURCES

INTRODUCTION

Each November, regional writing chapters and libraries across North America set up workshops and events around National Novel Writing Month—an annual, worldwide challenge in which writers attempt to write 50,000 words in 30 days. In 2021, after learning that I'd been a NaNoWriMo "failure" on two previous occasions, the adult programming coordinator at my local library asked if I'd consider hosting a virtual "debriefing" on November 30, titled *Failing (and Succeeding!) with NaNoWriMo*.

I agreed. If nothing else, it would encourage me to not only sign up for NaNoWriMo again, and make a concerted effort to reach the lofty 50,000-word mark for the fourth book in my *Marketville Mystery* series.

The 50,000 words didn't happen, though I did come close. Not that it mattered. It turned out the attendees—whether they'd written 50,000 words or not —were far more interested in the publishing process than drilling down on failing or succeeding at NaNoWriMo. Furthermore, the nature of their questions made me realize that the vast majority had absolutely no concept of how to proceed beyond NaNoWriMo. Hint: sending a 50,000-

word rough first draft to agents or publishers is *not* the way to proceed!

What really happens next?

I let that simmer for a few days, then approached the programming coordinator with an idea for a virtual presentation that would explore the pros and cons of various publishing options. She loved the concept, and we settled on a title—*Finding Your Path to Publication*—a date, and a timeline: five minutes for introductions, fifty-five minutes for the presentation, followed by a 30-minute Q&A. Because the event was virtual, it would be accessible to anyone who wanted to attend, even if they weren't a library patron or lived outside of the area.

Because the presentation contained so much information, I created a resource document with helpful links for the attendees, the kind of thing I would have loved when I was starting out. It didn't have all the answers, but it was a place to *start*.

Finding Your Path to Publication was both well attended and well received, leading to the creation of a spin-off presentation which was equally successful: *Self-Publishing: The Ins & Outs of Going Indie*.

Fast forward a couple of months, and the Independent Book Publishers Association (IBPA), of which I am a member, sent out a survey asking authors if they had any outside-the-box strategies for business development. I submitted my experience from my two presentations and less than a week later, the Managing Editor of *IBPA Independent* magazine asked if I'd be interested in penning an article for their May/June 2022 issue.

As a former freelance journalist, the idea of going back to my writing roots and sharing my experience held appeal, and so I agreed. Seeing that article in print also gave me another idea. Why not write a book that would demystify the publishing options available, including the steps required for each one? As a mystery author, I'm a complete pantser, never quite sure where the next chapter will lead, let alone the ending. With this project, I'd have my two presentations as an outline to follow.

The result is this book, but with one caveat: if you're looking for advice on which path you should choose, you won't find it here. One path does not fit all.

What you will find is a comprehensive, step-by-step guide to help you understand your options, including a breakdown of publishing and publishers: traditional (Big Five), independent (micro, small, medium, and large), hybrid/assisted, self, and social publishing. Included is information on editors and editing, writing a solid query letter, royalties, understanding copyright, and building your brand.

Throughout these pages, look for the (#AR) symbol, indicating a web link to more information in the Additional Resources section at the back of this book. In the same section, you'll also find Talking the Talk, a comprehensive reference list of terms frequently used in the publishing world.

And now it's time to turn the page and find *your* path to publication.

PAVING THE WAY

DEADLINES & DETAILS

One of the most common mistakes new authors make is sending their book "out there" before it's truly ready. Of course, the reverse is also true. I've heard of writers who have been editing and revising the same manuscript for years, never quite able to let it go. The question is, when is the time right, and how will you know when that time has arrived?

Arbitrary and Self-Imposed Deadlines

Maybe you've given yourself a timeline to get your project done, a milestone birthday or one year after retirement. Whatever the reason, arbitrary or self-imposed deadlines can be unrealistic. Yes, it's good to have a goal, a date to work towards. It's also important to allow yourself, and your book, the flexibility to change and adapt. Which brings us to…

Honest and Objective Feedback

Feedback comes in many forms and at various stages of the

writing process. The most important thing to remember is that you are looking for an honest and unbiased evaluation of your work. You won't agree with every comment or suggestion, but you should at least consider each one without becoming defensive. Consider it "thick skin" training for the rejections you're almost certain to face going forward. Let's look at some options:

WRITING CRITIQUE GROUPS

Writers who connect on a regular basis to share their work for the purpose of remaining accountable to their project, exchanging feedback, and improving their craft. While there are no hard and fast rules, these work best if the group is small—three to five people—allowing each member time to read and respond without becoming overwhelmed, while developing an ongoing and supportive relationship with one another.

Ideally, you'll also be working in the same genre. There's no point asking for feedback on your whodunit if your critique partner only reads historical romance and is unfamiliar with the tropes of cozy mysteries. It's also necessary to establish parameters from the get-go, including weekly word count limits and the type of feedback expected. Are you looking for big picture or line edits? Facebook, your local library, and writing associations can be great sources to find an established critique group or connect with people to form your own.

While critique groups can be invaluable for some writers, they should never be the final step in the review process. As you become immersed in your work for months on end, you will lose objectivity. Those intimately familiar with your work will too.

Critique groups also aren't for everyone. I've never belonged to one. Part of that is my own superstition: if I share it ahead of time, it won't come true. But mostly—at least when it comes to my fiction forays—it's because I prefer to focus solely on my work-in-progress without any intervention until the first, and sometimes the second, draft is complete.

Whatever path *you* choose while writing your novel, honest and objective feedback will be required at some point, and that point should be well understood before you start submitting your novel for representation or consider self-publishing. Writing means rewriting and multiple revisions. Be prepared to let go of your favorite passages, scenes, and characters if your readers and editors agree that they hinder the flow of the story. Conversely, you may have to create new passages and scenes to clarify motive and action.

Alpha Readers

Readers who provide detailed and constructive feedback, both positive and tactfully critical, about your book's premise, plot, characters, and other elements. Does the story flow, is it well paced, etc.? This is the place to include readers who have knowledge of the technical elements in your manuscript. You may have done extensive research and even if (for instance) appraising Irish bone china from the early Victorian era is your specialty, having a colleague fact-check your work will prove useful.

Whether you choose to hire a professional, or ask a trusted friend or relative, they should be aware that they are commenting on an unpolished (first) draft. They should also be avid readers of your book's genre or sub-genre.

While a critique group focuses on workshopping with other writers, consider this the first test drive of your overall story from a reader's perspective. This will help pinpoint any big picture problems that need to be addressed.

Beta Readers

Unlike alpha readers who provide first draft review, beta readers (or *betas*) critique finished manuscripts before they are published. As with alpha readers, it's advisable to have betas who are familiar with your genre/sub-genre.

Beta readers can be friends, family members, teachers, members of online writing groups, or other writers willing to do a manuscript swap—basically, anyone who will approach the book as a casual reader, pointing out things they liked and disliked. This will help identify the finer points of your book that may need an adjustment.

"Too many cooks spoil the broth," and this holds true when it comes to betas. Ideally, you'll have no fewer than two and no more than five, allowing for a comparison of opinions without the risk of opinion overload. If one beta reader doesn't understand why your protagonist hates red, that might be a point worth clarifying. If two or more betas don't get it, it's a must-fix.

While betas are an excellent way to obtain (usually free) feedback that allows you to tweak and polish your manuscript, they do not replace the role of a professional editor. There is one school of thought that because traditional publishers pay for editing, there is no need for authors to incur this expense if their intention is to traditionally publish.

Let's look at that statement. Is it true that traditional publishers hire and pay for editing services? Yes. However, it's equally true that agents and publishers receive thousands of submissions from aspiring authors every year. Furthermore, you only have one opportunity to submit to each agent and/or publisher on your wish list. While there are no guarantees, a professionally edited manuscript may increase the odds of acceptance.

On a personal level, I look at hiring the services of a professional editor as an investment in my personal publishing education. For example, I could sign up for creative writing class(es) or I could hire an editor to point out issues that are specific to my work, while helping me to learn and grow for about the same cost.

That said, if you are considering an assisted publishing model where editing and proofreading is part of a paid package, independent services may very well be an unnecessary expense. If you plan to self-publish, however, hiring an independent editor and proofreader is not a corner you want to cut.

Editing and Proofreading (#AR)

Just as there are genres and sub-genres in fiction, there are differences in the types of service editors provide. It's important to understand the nuances of each. Each editor is different, and many will provide a complimentary or modestly priced sample edit of a few pages, allowing both parties the opportunity to evaluate the relationship before signing a formal contract.

Developmental Editing

Also known as substantive or content editing, developmental editing is the first step, focusing on big picture story elements. The developmental editor will also assess and shape draft material to improve flow and organization by revising or reordering content and clarifying plot, arc of action, characters, and/or thematic elements.

Line Editing

Also known as stylistic editing, the line editor focuses on coherence and flow, eliminating jargon, clichés, and euphemisms, while adjusting the length and structure of sentences and paragraphs, and establishing or maintaining the overall mood, style, or voice.

COPYEDITING

Ideally combined with line editing, the copy editor checks spelling, grammar, punctuation, and usage, and ensures consistency in character names, places, descriptions, and other details. Copy editing also covers fact checking and/or obtaining or listing permissions needed (e.g., use of song lyrics or trademarked products). The copy editor may create or work from a style sheet.

PROOFREADING

Not to be underestimated, proofreading is the final step to catch errors (typos, punctuation, misplaced or missing modifiers, proper capitalization, consistency, and verb or tense usage) and ensure adherence to style. This is not the time to revise or rewrite. At this stage, you should have already completed any *necessary* revisions (though the urge to keep tweaking never truly stops). Proofreading is your final step to making sure your manuscript is clean and ready to be seen by others.

PUBLISHING PATHS

IF YOU'VE GOTTEN this far, you're clearly ready to put in the work. In this chapter, I'll do a quick overview on the types of publishing options available before delving into greater detail. These are not your only options; the publishing landscape is changing daily. But these are the ones we're going to explore and are, to the best of my knowledge, the most popular as of this writing. You'll also find that there are pros and cons to each path, though how you define those will depend on your individual needs, wants, and personality. For that reason, I've omitted a structured pros and cons list. After all, my pro may very well be your con.

TRADITIONAL (TRADE BOOK) A.K.A. THE BIG FIVE

Most aspiring authors dream of signing a contract with one of the "Big Five" traditional book houses (Hachette Book Group, HarperCollins, Macmillan Publishers, Penguin Random House, and Simon & Schuster), publishers with a team of professionals who take care of everything from editing, proofreading, interior book design, cover art, digital and/or print advance review copies

(ARCs), book blurbs and uploading to retail, to detailed sales reports to accompany royalty payments, and assistance with advertising and promotion.

Traditional publishers may also pay an advance against future royalties (the author's money to keep, even if the advance doesn't earn out), though in today's world advances aren't guaranteed with a book deal. The amount of an advance, if offered, is typically 50% on signing of the contract and 50% on publication, although terms can and do vary. The amount of the advance offered will depend on how much the publisher wants to publish your book. Authors with a bestselling track record and those with celebrity status or name recognition will reap the largest rewards.

Getting a book deal as an unknown author is far from easy. With rare exceptions, traditional houses do not accept manuscripts from authors directly and will only work with literary agents. This means you must first start the process of finding a reputable literary agent who will represent you and your book, an extensive process that can take months, even years. That's because reputable literary agents do not charge a reading or placement fee. They work on a commission basis, earning a percentage of your royalties (including advances) when you are paid. The good news: they *want* you to get paid, and work hard to make it happen. The bad news: they need to be selective about the clients they take on.

No matter how great your book is, if you're an unknown commodity without celebrity status, name recognition, or some sort of networking "in," you aren't likely to be at the top of anyone's wish list. So, when you're pitching your book to agents, your title needs to stand out to capture their attention. You'll learn more about this process in Getting Down to Business.

Patience is a definite virtue when it comes to landing a Big Five deal. Publication often takes 18 to 24 months from the day you sign on the dotted line, though it can, and often does, take much longer.

INDEPENDENT PUBLISHERS

If being traditionally published is important to you, regardless of your reasons, a contract with an independent publisher is often more attainable. That's because unlike trade book conglomerates, independent publishers (which will later be defined as micro, small, medium, or large press) accept manuscripts directly from the author without the aid of a literary agent, although you'll need to pay attention to their submission guidelines, which vary. In addition, they might have "open" and "closed" reading periods.

Regardless of the size of the press, your contractual agreement should, at a minimum, include paid professional editing, proofreading, cover art, interior book design, uploading to retail, and structured sales reports to accompany any royalty payments. Some will offer a modest advance (think in the low hundreds) against future royalties, again usually 50% on signing, 50% on publication. Other terms vary by press, but all should be clearly identified in the contract.

Some presses will offer digital ARCs (Advanced Reader Copies), though many do not, preferring to fast-track publication in lieu of sending out advance review copies. Authors may also be expected to solicit and/or pay for their own reviews through a review service, and the advertising and promotion budget and support is often minimal. The time from acceptance to publication tends to be faster than a traditional press, typically a few months to a year.

HYBRID / ASSISTED

Not to be confused with the term "hybrid author" (an author who is both traditionally and self-published), hybrid publishers offer assisted self-publishing, sometimes referred to as "pay-to-play." Years ago, these publishers were known as vanity presses, and there are still plenty of unethical vanity presses out there that will take an author's money and do little to nothing in return beyond getting your book out there, regardless of whether it's ready or marketable. When searching for a hybrid publisher, the importance of careful research cannot be overstated.

In many ways, a reputable hybrid publisher behaves much the same as a traditional publisher. They will vet submissions, publish under their own imprint and ISBNs (International Standard Book Number) (#AR), adhere to industry standards, and ensure editorial, design, and production quality. They will also publish in both print and digital formats, provide distribution services, and have demonstrated sales.

There are some notable differences, however. Where a traditional publishing company will assume all financial costs related to your book's publication (cover art, editing, interior book design, etc.), a hybrid publisher uses an author-subsidized business model in exchange for a higher-than-industry standard share of royalties. Expect a complete hybrid publishing package to cost several thousand dollars. A small percentage of authors recoup their investment. However, if you're interested in self-publishing without the responsibility of subcontracting editorial and design services, and without the learning curve to upload your book to retail, the hybrid model offers a viable, albeit expensive, alternative.

SELF-PUBLISHING

Self-publishing takes hard work, time, and commitment.

Years ago, the only way to self-publish was to use a hybrid publisher, but today it is easier than ever to upload your book to a variety of retailers and make it available for purchase by libraries and in online and brick-and-mortar bookstores. However, there are some caveats.

Where literary agents are looking for an author with name

recognition before investing their time and money, so too are booksellers, librarians, and readers. For the unknown author, gaining recognition in a very crowded and competitive marketplace can be an uphill battle, and not one for the faint of heart.

Another consideration is your own time, money, and organizational skills. As a self-published author, you essentially act as your own contractor, taking on, and paying for, all publishing-related responsibilities. That means editing, proofreading, cover art, interior page design, and more. While your costs will be significantly lower than going hybrid, they will be much higher than if you were to follow a traditional publishing route.

There are upsides, too. Unlike traditional publishing, where the publisher calls the shots (and often dictates the cover art), as an indie-publisher, you have complete control of your book's path to publication from start to finish. Furthermore, any royalties paid are yours and yours alone, no sharing with another party. That said, 100% of nothing is, well…still nothing. A quality product, along with a strong social media platform and marketing plan, are essential for return on your investment. Don't mistake "easier than ever" with easy.

If self-publishing sounds like more than you're willing to take on, and you're not sold on hiring a hybrid service, consider an independent publisher that offers distribution services in exchange for a percentage of your net sales, e.g., a 20% (publisher) 80% (author) split. One such example is Untreed Reads Publishing (#AR).

Social Publishing

Social publishing is an avenue for authors to write, publish, and distribute their work in a public or semi-public forum directly to readers, either by a personal blog or via an established storytelling website. Self-directed, the emphasis is on feedback and growth as a writer, and the pleasure of sharing your words, versus earning writing-based, royalty income.

Social publishing can allow authors to develop their voice while potentially building a fan base. It can also provide a forum to create longer works in a serialized format. It's important to note, however, that any work(s) shared in this matter will be considered previously published, significantly reducing, if not eliminating, any interest by traditional publishers and literary agents for those specific work(s). It will not, however, preclude the author from undertaking an independent or hybrid publication path for those same work(s).

MANAGING EXPECTATIONS

"Of all the learned professions, literature is the most poorly paid." — Dr. Edward Eggleston, 1890.

I KNOW what you're thinking…is she ever going to get to the part about finding my path to publication? I promise I will. But before I do, allow me to touch briefly on managing expectations. Yours, to be exact. Because the reality is, very few authors earn a living exclusively from their book royalties. If your primary motivation to get published is to get rich, you might want to consider another line of work.

The following data has been culled from two independent author income surveys, one from the Authors Guild, and the other from Sisters in Crime.

AUTHORS GUILD AUTHOR INCOME SURVEY

Founded in 1912, the Authors Guild is America's oldest and largest professional organization of writers, welcoming traditionally published authors and self-published authors alike in all genres and categories. From June 7 to August 21, 2018, the Authors Guild conducted a survey of U.S. professional writers, generating data from 5,067 book authors, including traditionally published (46%), self-published (27%), and hybrid (traditionally published and self-published) authors (26%). Using the prior year (2017) as the benchmark, 53% of respondents considered authoring books their primary occupation, spending half or more of their work time writing (#AR). This was further broken down by category:

- Genre fiction: 38%
- Academic: 22%
- Literary fiction: 18%
- Nonfiction: 18%
- Undefined: 4%

In addition to the Authors Guild, several other writers' organizations and independent publishing platforms participated in the survey: Romance Writers of America, Society of Children's Book Writers, Sisters in Crime, International Thriller Writers, Textbook and Academic Authors Association, National Association of Science Writers, American Society of Journalists and Authors, Association for Garden Communicators, Independent Book Publishers Association, PEN American Center, Authors Alliance, Next Big Writer, B&N Press, Authors Registry, Ingram Spark, Reedsy, and Lulu.

Of the part-time, full-time, traditionally published, self-published, and hybrid-published authors who were surveyed, the median income for book-related activities was $3,100 in 2017. For all writing-related activities (speaking engagements, ghostwriting, editing, translating works of other authors, teaching and/or presenting workshops on writing, etc.) the median was $6,080. Approximately 25% of all authors surveyed earned $0 in book-related income in 2017.

The Guild and several partners sent out a new U.S. author income survey in February 2023, which ran for approximately two months. Results will be analyzed and reviewed prior to public release later in 2023.

SISTERS IN CRIME: BUSINESS OF BOOKS SURVEY (2022)

While specific to the mystery genre and its member authors, another survey was completed by Sisters in Crime (SinC) in December 2021 (#AR). Formed in 1987 as an activist group with a goal of supporting the work of women crime writers and addressing imbalances in the publishing industry, SinC's mission has expanded to focus on the core values of advocacy, equality, inclusion, and community for all genders.

Titled the *Business of Books Survey Report (2022)*, the survey was open for one month in early 2022, with invitations sent to all members. Responses were submitted anonymously, respondents were allowed to skip any questions they preferred not to answer, and a free-response box was offered with every question. Over 400 members took the survey, which covered the following categories:

- Reading Activities
- Writing Activities
- Short Fiction and Non-fiction Publications
- Book-length Fiction and Non-fiction Publications
- Author Activities
- Member Identities

While only SinC members were eligible to participate, the complete survey is available free to non-members (#AR). Annual income-based results were recorded under Author Activities in three categories: Traditional (including independent publishers),

Indie (self-published), and Hybrid (both traditionally and self-published).

At the high end, 5% of all authors reported an income of more than $100,000, with an equal number of traditional and indie authors represented in that category. At the low end, 4% of all authors (3% traditional, 1% indie, 0% hybrid) earned nothing, with 22% of traditional and 41% of indie authors reporting an income of less than $1,000. Here's a breakdown of the rest:

- $1,000 - $9,999: 31% traditional, 30% indie, and 67% hybrid.
- $10,000 - $49,999: 27% traditional, 15% indie, 32% hybrid.
- $50,000 - $74,999: 9% traditional, 3% indie, 0% hybrid.
- $75,000 - $99,999: 1% traditional, 0% indie, 0% hybrid.

Sounds daunting, doesn't it? I'll be honest with you, it can be. But that doesn't mean you shouldn't follow your dreams.

After all, they can't go anywhere without you.

ORPHANS & OTHER REALITIES

REGARDLESS OF THE publisher's size or the length of time they've been in business, authors can find themselves "orphaned" through no fault of their own. "Orphaned" is a term used when an author's publishing contract is terminated. (This is not to be confused with "orphaned work," a term that refers to a book where copyright exists, but where the copyright owner is either unknown or cannot be located. The same term is applied to music, film, and works of art, anywhere that copyright applies and cannot be traced.)

How do authors become orphaned, and can it happen to anyone, even if they are a bestselling author with an ironclad contract? The answer is "a lot of reasons," and "yes."

The technical term is "reversion of rights," which means the publishing rights granted under the terms of the publishing contract are reversed and returned to the author. Once a reversion of rights is complete, the author is free to grant those rights to another publisher.

That's all fine and good, except for one thing: unless past sales numbers are strong enough to support it (think *USA Today* or

New York Times bestsellers) few publishers are willing to take on an orphaned author's previously published titles. This is especially true (and difficult) for authors who have a series on the go. For example, book 4 in the series may have been written but not yet published. Landing a publishing deal for books 1 to 3, plus book 4 (and possibly subsequent books), while not impossible, can be difficult.

Some authors merely accept that fate as inevitable and give up trying. Some even stop writing altogether. This always breaks my heart. Others persevere and either self-publish or eventually manage to sign with a new publisher. Still others concentrate their efforts on a fresh start and begin a new series.

I've personally been orphaned twice, and very nearly orphaned twice more. And that's just since 2015. In the first case, a multi-author publisher (who had been in business for fourteen years) was faced with the death of her father (a key employee), as well as her own declining, and often debilitating, health. The decision to revert publishing rights back to the individual authors was made from necessity. That didn't change the fact that I was left to find a new home for the published book 1 in my Marketville Mystery series, not to mention the completed, but not yet published, book 2.

Even so, I wasn't concerned. My debut novel in my Glass Dolphin Mystery series had launched in July 2015 by another publisher (let's call them Publisher A), and the sequel was in production and scheduled for spring release. I approached Publisher A, who had thus far been an exemplary partner, and explained my situation. Within a few months, book 1 in the Marketville series was re-released with revised formatting, minor changes, and a new cover.

The plan was to release the second Marketville book the following year, but before we got to the contract signing stage the first warning signs with Publisher A appeared. Delayed communication and royalty reports, ARCs promised, but not delivered, publication dates moved up, authors privately messaging one another with more questions than answers.

With the writing on the wall for a second time, I made the decision to start my own publishing imprint in February 2018—Superior Shores Press. By July, Publisher A announced they were ceasing operation and reversion of rights letters were dispatched. No one was surprised.

In both cases, I was paid all royalties owed in a timely manner. In the case of publisher insolvency, versus voluntary closure, that wouldn't necessarily be the case. I got lucky there.

The cover art and the formatted files were a different story. It turned out copyright for the covers belonged to the graphic artists who designed them, and the files were part of the contractual services (editing, proofreading, interior design) rendered. In other words, they still belonged to the now defunct publishers. Because the copyright for the material belonged to me, I was able to (painstakingly) recreate both manuscripts. Needless to say, it wasn't easy, and took a lot of time I would have preferred to spend writing Marketville 3.

And I was very nearly orphaned twice more. Back in June 2014 I pitched book 1 in the Glass Dolphin series to a publisher's representative at a writers' conference in Toronto. The representative asked for a full manuscript. Before I had the opportunity to send it, I was offered a contract by Publisher A, who'd also requested a full manuscript a few months prior. As you now know, Publisher A has since folded, and while the other publisher remains in business, they have since disbanded their mystery line, orphaning all their mystery authors in the process. Fate (or irony?) at its finest.

The second time was with a publisher I truly coveted. I loved the books in their catalog (of which I'd read many), the cohesively designed covers, the buzz they created, and the awards many of their authors either won or were shortlisted for. I'd even met the acquisitions editor on a few occasions at conferences and was thoroughly impressed. When I narrowly missed a publishing offer, I cried for hours and moped for days. Three years later, that coveted publisher shuttered its doors.

The reality is that many authors I've known, read, and admired (including award-winning and *USA Today* bestselling authors) have been orphaned. Sometimes it's due to a publisher's personal circumstances. Sometimes publishers merge or get acquired and the list must be "culled." It's never personal, even if it feels that way. Don't let the doubt or fear of what "might happen" allow you to give up or discourage you from trying. There's always another light at the end of the tunnel, even if it's not the light you were expecting.

Eyes wide open. Head over heart. Believe.

GETTING DOWN TO BUSINESS

FIVE FIRST STEPS

WHATEVER PUBLISHING path you choose to undertake, there are a few critical first steps to help set yourself up for success. I've broken these down into five main categories: record keeping, writing your author bio, developing a social media platform, building a website, and defining your book.

RECORD-KEEPING

Being an author might sound glamorous, but if you've written a book you already know that it takes hard work and plenty of discipline. Furthermore, your chosen path might change over time. My best advice is to treat this journey like you're the sole proprietor of a business. From the day you decide you want to be a writer, turn up for work and write, network with other authors, and create a budget.

At a minimum, you'll want to keep all receipts and maintain a record of all your writing-related expenses. Think printer ink, paper, pens, computer purchases, software programs such as Microsoft Office or Scrivener, applicable postage and courier charges, webinars and educational courses, internet and cellular phone costs, professional services such as editing, conference or convention fees (including travel, hotel accommodation, and meals), and writing association dues. If you are working out of your home, a portion of business-use-of-home expenses (heat, hydro, water, property taxes, insurance, etc.) are often eligible for write-off.

It is also a good idea to keep a vehicle log. Include the starting and ending odometer readings for the year, as well as the date, return distance, and purpose of any writing-related trip. Going to the library to research historic archives? Need to make a trip to the office supply store for toner cartridge? Track it. The log should also include the cost of gasoline, vehicle maintenance, insurance, vehicle leasing or financing costs if applicable, and so on.

Consult with an accountant to guide you through the tax implications of startup, including what you can and can't write off, and whether or not you should apply for a tax number, set up a separate bank account, and how to register a business name/publishing imprint. While tax rules and regulations vary by location, the consultation fee and any business-related fees you pay an accountant for tax advice, setting up or keeping the business's books, and preparing a business tax return will be tax deductible (#AR).

WRITING YOUR AUTHOR BIO

This is always written in the third person and should be succinct and relevant, including as many of the following points as appropriate:

- Recent writing-related publications and/or positions.
- Expertise in the field of your book (this is especially relevant with non-fiction).

- Memberships in any writing associations or organizations.
- A minor personal detail: He lives in North Carolina with his wife and two children. If your book is a memoir, you would expand on that by adding something along the lines of, *Book Title* is based on his life on the road with his father, an itinerant musician.
- Website URL.

Of course, not everyone has writing-related publications, and that's okay. Here's an example of how to keep it simple:

Jane Doe is the author of Book Title *and an avid reader of fantasy novels. A member of Science Fiction and Fantasy Writers Association (SFWA), Jane lives in North Carolina with her husband and two children. Find out more at www.janedoe.com.*

I'll be addressing social media platforms next, but this also touches on another point which will be addressed later: if there is a local or regional writing association you can join, especially specific to your genre, it is invariably worth the price of admission. Belonging to one or more of these groups tells agents, publishers, and readers that you take your role as an author, and the craft of writing, seriously. For example, I belong to the Independent Book Publishers Association, Sisters in Crime, the Short Mystery Fiction Society, International Thriller Writers, and Crime Writers of Canada, where I served on the Board of Directors for five years, the last two as Chair.

DEVELOPING A SOCIAL MEDIA PLATFORM

It's never too early to start building your social media platform. In fact, agents and publishers will expect you to have an online presence. You don't have to do it all and be everywhere, but rather that you find a lane (or lanes) where you feel comfortable sharing pieces of yourself—at least as it pertains to writing and books.

Because the social media landscape is ever-changing, you'll also need to do your research. Do your books cater to teens and tweens, or older adults? What site is your target demographic most likely to follow? What are their expectations? Video clips or reels? Photo collages? Book reviews? Pictures of your cat or dog? How often should you post? The more you drill down into what works and what doesn't, the more successful you'll be at building your own following.

But social media isn't a one-way street. To be successful at it, you'll need to be a good member of the literary community. It's important to follow and tag writing associations you're affiliated with, as well as other authors—not just the big names or award winners, but those who, like you, may be just starting out. Share, comment, and like others' posts. Learn about hashtags (the best way to do this is by studying others). In short, treat your social media platform like homework, because unless you're already skilled at social media and self-promotion, you've got a steep learning curve ahead of you.

BUILDING A WEBSITE (#AR)

You may not think you're ready but whatever path you choose, your online presence should also include a website, however basic.

There are two ways of going about this. One is to hire a website developer and the other is to use a do-it-yourself website builder, of which there are many. The fun part will be coming up with, and registering, your domain name. More on that in a bit but get your thinking cap on and start googling to make sure "your" domain name isn't already in use. Ideally, a domain name will be your name (plus an extension like .com), but if you have a common first and last name, you'll have to get more creative. That's okay, but don't get so creative you lose your identity. For example, www.JaneDoeCozyAuthor.com could work, whereas www.CozyAuthorJane.com could be anyone.

Now let's take look at your options:

Hiring a developer

Probably the easiest approach, it will also be the most expensive.

If you do choose to hire a website developer, it's important to fully understand what that process will entail. Will you have complete control of the website once it's built, able to update and add content quickly and easily yourself? If not, will the developer retain responsibility for some, or all, of the updates? What is included in web developer services vary from one provider to the next. Some offer a set number of maintenance hours in your monthly or annual charge, with work over and above offered at an hourly rate, while others simply charge on a cost-per-change basis.

There's no right or wrong answer here, though the fine print is important. You may want to hand the whole thing off to an expert and be more than happy to do so. Or it might be more appealing to you to take complete charge once the basic structure is set up. Many web developers are open to that and are usually willing to provide additional guidance if required in future.

Only you know the answer that works for you. Just ensure that those answers are fully understood by both parties *and* are covered off in any contractual agreement.

DIY Approach

The second, less expensive, but more time-consuming, option

is to use a do-it-yourself website builder. (Don't worry, you won't need to learn how to write code or transform yourself from writer to techie.) And while this is a DIY approach, the end result doesn't need to look amateurish.

Choosing the website builder best suited to you depends on your wants and needs. You'll need to think about what you need now, but don't forget to also consider what you might require down the road so your website can grow with you, rather than having to start from scratch. Start by visiting the websites of authors who write in the same genre as you, and of authors whose work you admire, but again, don't just go with the big names. Check out online bookstores for novels in your genre written by lesser-known authors, then check out their websites as well. Chances are many will have gone the DIY route, and you'll often be able to tell by an imprint and links at the bottom of the page, "Powered by…" or "Developed with…."

Some websites will include a notation with the theme as well as the builder, helpful if you like one particular look (every website builder offers a variety of themes—templates you can build on). For example, my website, www.judypenzsheluk.com, includes "Designed by Elegant Themes / Powered by WordPress" in the footer.

Next, make a wish list of the things you'd like to see on your own website. Not everything needs to be done the first day you go live but can be added as time and energy permits. It's more than okay to start with a basic, functional website, as long as the theme and builder you select allow for future adaption based on your wish list.

Regardless of your wish list, one important consideration (since it's usually one or the other) is your website's landing page —the page readers are taken to when entering your URL. Do you want a home (welcome) page separate from your blog? Or do you prefer that readers land directly on your most recent post? Do you even want a blog? You should also decide whether you'll be using your website as an e-commerce site, selling books and any related merchandise direct to consumer.

The good news is that most website builders offer free trial accounts. Take advantage of that opportunity, and don't worry while you test out various options—your website won't be live until it's activated, so no one will be able to see it but you.

Another consideration is what the website builder offers in terms of registering your domain name and website hosting options. Prices vary for website hosting, so shop around. Keep in mind, there's usually a deal to be made if you're a new customer (including free domain name registration). Website hosting is typically billed on an annual basis; regardless of the deal you make, be sure to review the renewal rates since these can escalate significantly over time. You'll also want to select a host that offers 24/7 technical support via phone and chat. Trust me, when something goes wrong, you want to know that someone will be available to help you fix it quickly. The last thing you want is to lose sales or visitors because of technical difficulties.

Feeling daunted? The internet is your friend when it comes to researching what's out there, and trustworthy online comparisons by industry professionals are a great way to understand the pros and cons of the various services.

Defining your Book

Think of your book in terms of real estate. If you were selling your home, the listing would include the type of house—detached, semi-detached, townhouse, condo hi-rise, etc.—the number of bedrooms and bathrooms, location, and any other special or unique features. When setting the price, your agent would look for comparable units, both past and present.

Defining your book is much the same, starting with a main category and further defined by sub-categories. A cozy mystery about a female amateur sleuth that works in a restaurant could be categorized as follows: FICTION / Mystery & Detective / Amateur Sleuth, FICTION / Mystery & Detective / Cozy / Culinary, and FICTION / Mystery & Detective / Women Sleuths. If you plan to self-publish, Book Industry Standards and Communications (BISAC) codes will be required at retail upload (more information in Understanding Your Options: Self-publishing), but when it comes to categorizing your book, a review of BISAC codes (listed on their website) is a great place to start (#AR).

If you plan to pitch your book to agents and/or publishers, it's your responsibility to sell them on your book using the appropriate categories, in this case, as a "cozy, culinary mystery about a sous chef who discovers a dead body in the deep freezer. When suspicion falls on her, she resorts to sleuthing to clear her name." I've included more examples under Securing an Agent or Publisher / Loglines later in this section.

Being able to compare your novel to bestselling books that are similar can also help paint a picture but refrain from boasting or making grandiose claims (these scream amateur). A simple statement, such as "similar in style to *Title* by *Author* with humorous undertones and a feisty, likable protagonist" will suffice.

What if your book isn't quite so easy to define as that? I'd like to tell you it doesn't matter, but that's not the reality. If you can't define your book, then no one else will be able to either. That includes agents, publishers, booksellers, and librarians. In short, this is not the time to try to invent a new category.

Hey, if this were easy, everyone would do it.

UNDERSTANDING COPYRIGHT

COPYRIGHT LAW PROVIDES protection for a variety of artistic pursuits, everything from literary to performance to musical works. This chapter will deal exclusively with copyright as it applies to literary works, though I'd be remiss if I didn't mention that you *cannot* use song lyrics in your work (unless it is in the public domain)—not so much as a single line—without express written permission, and more often than not, a *lot* of money. You can, however, reference a song *title* (since the title of any written work cannot be copyrighted). In other words, it's okay to write, "Blue Rodeo's 'Five Days in May' was playing softly in the background."

You should be equally wary of quoting segments from any other copyrighted material, including novels (though once again, referencing a book's title is acceptable). The disclaimers included on the copyright page of a book are meant to be taken seriously. The Berne Convention for the Protection of Literary and Artistic Works, an international treaty ratified by 175 countries (including the United States and Canada) and administered by the World Intellectual Property Organization (WIPO) ensures that copyright is respected in those countries, regardless of where the copyright was filed (#AR).

So, what is copyright? Simply defined, it means just what it says— "the right to copy." The copyright holder (that's you, the author) owns the exclusive right to produce or reproduce your own *original* work, in whole or in substantial part. If the work is unpublished (as yours will be when submitting to agents and publishers), copyright includes the right to publish or grant publishing rights for the work and/or any substantial part of it.

As the copyright holder, you are also automatically protected by copyright at the time of creation, with the following provisions:

- You are a citizen or resident of a treaty country included in The Berne Convention for the Protection of Literary and Artistic Works (#AR). Both the United States and Canada are members.
- The work is first published in a treaty country even if, as the author, you were not a citizen or resident in one of the treaty countries.

Knowing that, you might wonder why you would apply, and pay for, copyright registration, and what you might receive back in return. Not a lot, to be honest, although you will receive a certificate of registration protecting your work, which can be used in court to prove ownership of your book, should the need arise. And yes, you can always frame the certificate to hang in your office. Note: Copyright should always be filed under your legal name, not your publishing imprint or pen name. The exception would be if you were an incorporated business. For example, the copyright listed on bestselling author Michael Connelly's books is Hieronymus, Inc.

There are some exceptions to copyright law, but the biggie is that you cannot copyright a title. That's why you'll see books and movies with the exact same title. That said, titles are important, and the last thing you want is one too closely associated with a universally known classic.

How long does copyright last? In the U.S., copyright protection for authors of an original work exists during your lifetime and for seventy years following your death. In Canada, the term is lifetime plus fifty years. Different rules apply for anonymous works or works for hire.

That also brings up the question of who owns your copyrighted work(s) after you die. In general, as with other property you own, ownership of your copyrighted work will be transferred to the heir(s) of your estate, unless you specify another individual in your will. Once ownership has been passed on, the new owner may generally use and license your works in whatever way they wish, in the same way they can sell or dispose of any of your other belongings. It's best to discuss this with a lawyer specializing in estate law and should be part of the conversation when you're preparing your will.

In closing, there is no need to add the copyright symbol © to your manuscript when submitting it for consideration to an agent or publisher. Doing so will only highlight that you are an amateur. All contracts and direct-to-retail uploads will include a clause where you certify that you are the rightful owner of the copyright. No one else, not your publisher, agent, or retailer, owns the copyright to your work, published or unpublished.

SECURING A LITERARY AGENT OR PUBLISHER

Before we get into the nuts and bolts of traditional publishing, I'm going to address first steps. Whether you are seeking agent representation, or taking your pitch directly to a publisher, there are some commonalities you'll need to be prepared for: submission guidelines, loglines, query letters, writing a synopsis, and managing submissions.

Submission Guidelines

Included on an agency or publisher's website, submission guidelines are the instructions that tell you the type of books they accept and how they want your work sent for consideration. They may be called guidelines but consider these hard and fast rules. You are now entering the business side of the writing world, and this is not the time to display your creativity or unique take on things.

This is also the time to READ CAREFULLY. You might be thinking, no problem. I'll format my material once and have my package ready for mass mailing. If that's the case, you might be frustrated at first to find that there are many small differences in these guidelines from one agency to the next. This is intentional. The reason? Your submission is your application in more ways than one. Agencies and publishers don't only want to see your writing, they want to make sure you can follow instructions and pay attention to details—all things that will give them an idea of whether you would be someone they can consider going into business with.

Pro Tip: Don't pick and choose which submission guidelines you want to follow. You might be tempted to leave your margins the way they are, but even one thing can be a red flag for the person on the other end of your submission.

Now, you might be thinking "it goes without saying," and you'd think so, wouldn't you? Yet from my personal experience as publisher of the Superior Shores Anthologies, I can assure you that is often not the case. Let's look at some examples based on my submission guidelines, and how that might relate to your own submission process:

Formatting: Word document (.doc or .docx), Times New Roman font size 12, double spaced, 1" margins, .5" indent (no tabs), no header or footer (yes, that means no page numbers).

- I received a couple of PDFs, a variety of fonts (Calibri, as I recall, was quite popular, likely because it is the default for Mac users), and several documents with either a header or a footer. The PDFs were returned without being read. The other submissions weren't rejected, but I wondered if the author would be difficult to work with. If the authors couldn't or wouldn't follow formatting instructions, what would they be like when it came to editing?

Another element of submission guidelines you are likely to

see includes a wish list, such as this one included in my Call for Submissions for *Moonlight & Misadventure*:

"Sub-genres: Traditional, locked room, noir, historical, humorous, and suspense will be considered; however, do not submit stories with overt sex, violence, or bad language. Speculative fiction, sci-fi, fantasy, and paranormal are **not** of interest for this collection. And please, no werewolves. We really do not care for werewolves."

- I received a couple of sci-fi, one submission that could only be classified as erotica, another loaded with f-bombs, and one story about werewolves that promised to be "different." Each story was rejected without further consideration, including the sci-fi entry which, while well written, simply would not have fit with the overall collection (hence the notation in the guidelines).

Let's look at that from the perspective of an agent or publisher. If their guidelines (or their website) clearly state that they don't accept certain genres or sub-genres and your novel falls into that category, it's time to move on. No matter how polished your manuscript is, you're wasting their time, and your own.

Word count: 1,500 to 5,500 words (though great stories falling "slightly" outside this range will be considered).

- Perhaps the "slightly outside" wasn't definitive enough, however, a story at 750 or 7,500 words pushed the boundaries beyond reasonable limits. There's being flexible, and then there's being an Olympic gymnast.

Would a larger or less forgiving agent or publisher reject a submission because of these discretions? Not necessarily, but it happens. But even if they might be willing to overlook the formatting, why take the chance? Showing respect for the submission guidelines is the first step in demonstrating that you are a professional. And since publishing is hard enough, wouldn't it be better to take a few extra minutes to make sure you're giving yourself the best chance? If you're doing all this work, the last thing you want is for your submission to get rejected without even being read, all because you've sent the wrong format. Be careful, and you'll be showing respect for their time and yours.

Each agent or publisher will have different submission directives. Few will ask for the full manuscript in the first round, rather, they'll want a sample of what's in store: first 50 pages, first three chapters, first 10,000 words, and so on. If you've piqued their interest, you should get a request for a "partial" (the first so-many-words or chapters) and if you've hit it out of the park, a "full" (complete manuscript).

A not-so-subtle reminder: if the formatting, partial, or full request is Times New Roman 12 with 1" margins, do not change it to Times New Roman 11 or narrow the margins to increase the number of chapters you can jam into 50 pages. If your chapter ends at page 48 or 49 and it's a good place to leave the story, then it's acceptable to submit a page or two less.

*Pro Tip: If formatting guidelines are not provided, the industry standard is Times New Roman 12, 1" margins all around, double-spaced, with page numbers in the footer, and the author's last name/abbreviated title in header as follows: Penz Sheluk/Plans. Indent the first line of a paragraph at .5" (and don't use the space bar or tab key to do it). The easiest way to do this is to set up auto format parameters in the Format / Paragraph toolbar section of Word.

Loglines (#AR)

Imagine that you're in an elevator and an influential person standing next to you says, "Pitch me your book." (Hey, this is your dream, right?) You've got thirty, maybe sixty, seconds, before the doors open. What would you say?

Let's consider another, maybe more likely scenario: you're at a writing conference, one that offers agent pitch sessions. Five minutes or less to convince them to take a chance on you. Perhaps you're doing a pitch contest on Twitter, trying to stand out from the (very crowded) crowd. Or maybe you've decided to indie publish and you're prepping your social media posts to self-promote your book.

Whatever the case might be, you've got one to two sentences max to get the attention of an agent/publisher/potential reader and hook them. Enter the "logline," also known as an "elevator pitch."

Loglines are big business in Hollywood. The good news is that even though you're writing a book, not a screenplay, you can learn from them. Can you guess the name of these popular films based on the logline?

1. "After a tornado whisks a Kansas farm girl to the land of Oz, she embarks on a journey to meet a wizard in the hope of getting back home."
2. "An airhead blonde goes to Harvard Law School."
3. "Two star-crossed lovers fall in love on the maiden voyage of the Titanic and struggle to survive as the doomed ship sinks into the Atlantic Ocean."
4. "A cowboy doll is profoundly threatened and jealous when a new spaceman action figure supplants him as top toy in a boy's room."
5. "The lives of two mob hit men, a boxer, a gangster's wife, and a pair of diner bandits intertwine in four tales of violence and redemption."

What do these five examples have in common? (After all, we know it's not genre.) Let's drill it down:

- Each one conveys the premise in a single sentence.
- None of the characters are named.
- There is no mention of a sub-plot and, unlike a synopsis (more on that later), no nod to the ending.

In summary, a logline needs to be concise, ideally conveying the essence of your plot in one, and no more than two, sentences. You must, however, reference your protagonist in some way, and possibly your antagonist and/or the obstruction(s) to their goal. In our first example, you could add, "Along the way, she befriends a tin man, lion, and scarecrow searching for their own salvation, only to be stopped by a wicked witch along the way."

Like every other part of your writing journey, perfecting loglines takes perseverance, patience, and lots and lots of practice. Fortunately, there are a multitude of books, movies, and television shows to practice on, even if you're the only one who's ever going to read (or appreciate) your efforts. Then again, you might make it a game to play with a friend, family member, or critique group.

And now the answers to our logline quiz:

1. *The Wizard of Oz*
2. *Legally Blonde*
3. *Titanic*
4. *Toy Story*
5. *Pulp Fiction*

But you already knew that, didn't you?

QUERY LETTERS

APPROACH your quest for representation the same way you'd approach a prospective employer. Treat the query letter like a cover letter and the submission guidelines and agent/publisher's wish list like the requirements in a job ad.

Most literary agents expect writers to query multiple agents at the same time, though there are exceptions. One example is if the agency's submission guidelines specifically state they prefer that writers avoid simultaneous submissions. Another is if the agent requested an *exclusive* look at your submission at a writing conference or online pitch session (not all direct requests are exclusive). Any specific terms should be clarified at the time of the request.

If you are submitting because of an invitation, your query letter should serve as a reminder, with details of the meeting/session date, place, and terms of the request. (Agents meet a lot of people, and your meeting likely won't stick as clearly in their mind as it does yours.)

Additionally, if your submission is on an exclusive basis, be sure to include a reasonable timeline to protect you from waiting indefinitely for a response. That timeline may be offered on the agent's website (for example, "We respond to all queries within 30 days,") or it may have been part of the pitch session negotiations. If you are left wondering, I'd suggest a period of no less than four and no more than eight weeks. You might not get a response (this is much more common than you might think), but it gives you an opportunity to follow up in a professional and courteous manner. In the follow up, indicate that while you remain very open to working with them, you will now begin querying other agents. This kind of notification is fair to both parties, serving both as a gentle reminder to the agent (which might prompt a response) and as permission for you to continue the process.

Here are a few e-mail query Do's and Don'ts:

DO: Make it clear why you are contacting them, whether through an online form or by email (few agents accept snail mail submissions these days). Follow any submission guideline requirements for the subject line. If one isn't specified, enter "Query, TITLE." If your query is in response to a pitch session request, add, "As per your request." If you've been referred to them by one of their client's, add, "Jane Doe Client Referral." E.g., Query, TITLE, Joe Doe Client Referral.

DON'T: Add extraneous information to the subject line. If there is no referral or pitch session to reference, a simple "Query, TITLE" will suffice.

DO: Address the agent by name and, above all, spell it correctly! Unless you've met the agent personally or via an online pitch session, refer to them formally. In the past, the recommendation would have been to use an honorific (Mr., Ms.) but first names are not always an easy clue to gender, nor does it address the increase in visibility and awareness for non-binary identities. As such, the new standard is to address as First Name Last Name (spell it correctly!). Remember, this is a business communication, not an email to a friend. It is always better to err on the side of professionalism.

DON'T: Address the letter "To Whom it May Concern," or worse, "Dear Literary Agent."

DO: Get straight to the point, e.g., "Jane Doe, I am seeking representation for my [word count] cozy mystery titled TITLE (uppercase, no italics). I believe this novel would be a good fit for your agency because [enter your reason here]."
By entering the word count (which will fall inside the parameters

of the submission guidelines) and by giving a reason (something that directly speaks to the agent's wish list), you are showing that you've done your homework.

DON'T: Get gimmicky and write in the voice of your character.

DO: Include your logline, followed by a brief summary (no more than two paragraphs) of your book.

DON'T: Tell the agent your book has been professionally edited; that is already the assumption and highlights that you are an amateur.

DO: Introduce comparables, e.g., "I believe TITLE would appeal to readers of author Jane Doe and her *such-and-such* (italics) cozy mystery series. Note: If the agent represents Jane Doe, all the better, as it once again shows that you've done your homework. Keep comparables down to two or three.

DON'T: Make grandiose claims about how your book is as good as or better than those comparables, or that you're sure that the agent will love your writing.

DO: Read any comparables you reference, just to be sure your book is truly similar in style.

DON'T: Trust back of book blurbs in your search for comparables.

DO: Provide a brief paragraph about yourself, including any pertinent facts. A paramedic might use their knowledge in a medical mystery, a horticulturalist a knowledge of poisonous plants.

DON'T: Include personal information, such as your age, sex, religion, marital status, number of children, etc., unless one or more of these facts are directly relevant to your novel.

DO: End with a professional courtesy, such as "Thank you for your time and consideration," and a call to action, "I look forward to hearing from you." Finish with a "sincerely" or an "all the best," and if emailing (vs. completing an online form) include your full name, telephone number (optional, but advisable), and website URL, if applicable.

DON'T: Make demands, such as, "I expect to hear from you in sixty days," even if the agent's website states that sixty days is their typical turnaround time.

And one final DON'T: Submit more material than requested in the submission guidelines. There's also no need to state you are following the guidelines. That's a given.

While some agents and publishers still accept e-mail queries, more and more are using an online query management system to track queries. In addition to your material, these online forms will request some or all of the following: Name, e-mail address, biography, website, Twitter or other Social Media handle, phone number. You can also expect to answer questions such as: Have you previously published other books? Been previously represented by another agent? Who (name of agent/agency)? Name of referral (if applicable).

The online form will also have a "Tell us about your book" section. This is where you'll copy and paste your text (pay attention to any special formatting guidelines), and enter your query letter, logline, and similar books.

Remember that you've spent months, possibly years, working on your manuscript. Take the time you need to craft a professional query letter, personalized in some way for every agent you approach. It won't be a guarantee of success, but at least you'll have given it your all.

Still unsure? Google "successful query letters" or check out QueryLetter.com for 161 examples of queries that worked (#AR).

WRITING A SYNOPSIS

What is a synopsis, exactly? Derived from the Ancient Greek word *synopsesthai*, meaning "a comprehensive view," a synopsis is exactly that: a summary of your novel's narrative arc, including plot twists and the ending, as well as brief descriptions of major characters. I don't mean details like hair or eye color, unless that's significant to the plot, but rather personality traits that define the character. Take *The Wizard of Oz* as an example. It doesn't matter if Dorothy has auburn hair worn in braids, but it does matter that she's a naïve farm girl from Kansas, a stranger in a strange land. Last, but not least, a synopsis is not the same as a back of the book or retail blurb; spoilers are an expected part of the package.

If there's one benefit to following a non-traditional publishing path, it's that you won't have to write a synopsis. I say that because writing a succinct and compelling synopsis is far from easy. That doesn't mean you need to hire a synopsis writer, though there are writers who specialize in doing just that. Costs for this service vary widely and can be charged on a flat fee or hourly basis. When choosing who to work with, you'll want to make sure the writer's expertise is in synopsis writing for novels rather than scholarly articles or research projects. Ideally, the writer will provide a sample synopsis (free or for a nominal fee) of the first one to three chapters of your novel so you can get a feel for their style and ability level. There are also online courses to help you learn the skill yourself. Review the curriculum to ensure the focus is on synopses for novels before enrolling.

Your synopsis should be:

- Single spaced.
- Between 500 and 800 words (unless otherwise stated in submission guidelines).
- One to two pages, using standard font and sizes, e.g., Times New Roman 12, with normal (1") margins.
- Written in the third person, present tense (even if your book is written in first person, past tense).
- Clear, concise, and neutral in tone. Unlike your novel, you want to TELL not SHOW.

Other synopsis standards include:

- Putting the title at the top of the page, e.g., *Skeletons in the Attic*: Synopsis, with your name on the line below.
- Naming your file with your novel's name_synopsis.doc, e.g., Skeletons-in-the-Attic_synopsis.doc (or abbreviated as SITA_synopsis.doc), vs. simply "synopsis"—you want your document to stand out.
- Putting main character names in uppercase (most common) or bold font (acceptable) when first introduced, along with their age in parentheses and a brief description, e.g., Single city girl CALAMITY (CALLIE) BARNSTABLE (36) inherits a house in Marketville with the proviso she move into the house and investigate her mother's murder thirty years before.
- Keeping setting details to a minimum while painting the picture, e.g., *Skeletons in the Attic* is set in Marketville, the sort of town where families with two

kids, a collie, and a cat move to for a bigger house, a better school, and soccer fields.

- Limit the number of named characters. Your protagonist and antagonist, and if applicable, sidekick(s), are essential. Beyond that, it's better to write "the bartender," vs. "the bartender, BETSY EHRLICH." When it comes to the synopsis, less is more.

There are any number of ways to begin but approaching your initial attempt as a first draft can alleviate the pressure. Without worrying about word count, here are a couple of ways to do that:

1. Write one, and no more than two, explanatory sentences for each chapter. What is the chapter's purpose or pivotal scene? That's what you're trying to capture, no more and no less. Let's say the average per chapter is 20 words (as are the first two sentences of this bullet point, to give you a quick reference point). With 50 chapters, you'd be looking at 1,000 words. Over your target, yes, but on review you'll look for elements that, while important to the novel, can be excluded in your synopsis.

2. Tell the story from beginning to end in the same way you might tell the story to a friend over coffee. This is a talking-out-loud exercise, and you'll want to record yourself using your phone or computer. You'll probably find yourself stopping and restarting, and that's okay. Then transcribe the recording into a Word document, and let the editing begin.

As FAR AS the structure of your synopsis, you'll want to include major plot points in the following order:

- Introduction of your protagonist and their mindset/current world, addressing the five "W's. (Who/what/when/where/why).
- Reveal the inciting incident while emphasizing the protagonist's motivation. In *The Wizard of Oz,* Dorothy wants to get home to Kansas. The Wicked Witch of the West wants to stop her.
- Continue with the rising action or sequence of events that build tension until you reach the height of the action (also referred to as the crisis or climax), at which point the protagonist typically decides on a course of action or faces the truth.
- Conclude with the falling action (denouement), tying up loose ends to reach the final resolution, closing both plot and narrative arc.
- Restate the protagonist's motivation (Dorothy finds her way home).

Here are a few simple do's and don'ts:

DO: Introduce major characters in order of appearance.

DON'T: Get bogged down with sub-plots and secondary characters.

DO: Touch on the overarching theme of your novel without getting too deep into the weeds. Let's use *The Wizard of Oz* once again, which includes several underlying themes, each important to the story. However, if you were limited to one, either good versus evil or the power of friendship would work.

DON'T: Include dialogue. Remember you are relating the story in a factual manner.

DO: Touch on the genre/sub-genre of your book while making every word count, e.g., "a fast-paced political thriller" can be boiled down to "a political thriller" because, by definition, thrillers are fast-paced.

DON'T: Add unnecessary details. It doesn't matter if your character favors blue because it matches her eyes.

DO: Run your synopsis by one or two beta readers before sending it out.

DON'T: Ask rhetorical questions, e.g., "Calamity is faced with a decision. What would you do?"

Summing up 80,000 words into 800 or less can be a challenge, but don't let that intimidate you. It's all about taking it one step, and one version, at a time.

Managing Submissions

There are subtle differences between Agent Submissions and Publisher Submissions, and tips that are applicable to both. Even if your preference is strongly skewed to one path or the other, don't let your personal bias or desire stop you from considering every angle.

Agent Submissions (#AR)

Start by compiling a master list of agents currently accepting submissions that meet your criteria (genre/sub-genre and word count). I like to use an Excel spreadsheet, but you may find it easier to use a Word document, or an online program, such as QueryTracker.net or PublishersMarketplace.com (but realize online resources will not have all agents/publishers in their databases).

It's also important to note that it's considered bad form to query two agents from the same agency, which makes sense. Would you send your CV to two managers at one company for the same position? Of course not.

Because this is your master list, it should include the names of thirty to fifty agents, ranked or sorted in the order of your preference. I know that sounds like a lot of names, but if you're already doing the homework, you may as well compile a list worthy of the effort. In fact, I'd encourage you to compile a separate list of agents/agencies you'd considered, but eliminated, with the reason for your decision. At the very least it will save you from retracing your steps.

Your master list should include the name of the agency, the agent's first and last name, website URL, and a brief note on their guidelines (first three chapters, first 50 pages, one-page synopsis, etc.). Additionally, you'll want a column for the date you sent your submission, date acknowledged (not all agents will acknowledge receipt), and a Y/N for their response.

If it's a no: Include any feedback, such as whether it was a form letter or a personalized rejection. Form letter rejections are easy to spot because they tend to be generic in the wording. A personalized rejection will include references to your novel and/or query letter. While a rejection will sting, any advice or suggestions offered can only serve to assist you going forward, and a positive comment or two can make it sting a little less. Resist the urge, however strong, to respond, unless, and *only* unless, the agent has invited any questions or comments. Instead, cross that agent off your list and move on to the next.

If it's a yes: Do a happy dance, then record the response for a full or partial manuscript and reply promptly with the requested material, submitted in the manner they request (font, spacing, etc.). Update your submission log accordingly. If they ask for an exclusive, refer to the query letter section that addresses this and follow the same process. If they don't ask for an exclusive, keep on querying. It can take several months to a year (or sometimes more) to hear anything back, and although you've cleared a massive hurdle, it still might be a rejection.

Now, you might be thinking: what if this is my dream agent, and another agent offers me a contract before I hear back? The good news is this provides a legitimate opportunity to follow up with Agent #1. Advise them that while they remain your top pick, you have received an offer from another agent, and would therefore request an update on the status of your submission. They should either bow out or jump in, though they may still be months away from a final decision. At that point, it's up to you to decide whether to go for a sure thing or hold out for the dream. As far as communicating with Agent #2, not only is it acceptable to ask for two weeks to review and consider the offer, it's expected and advisable. I'll cover contracts off in greater detail in Money Matters.

The prevailing wisdom is to send queries out in batches of six to eight. There's good reason for this—if your initial batch is met with some positive response, you've got the first step down. Conversely, if your first batch is rejected without a single request for additional material, and worse, only with form letter rejections, odds are your query letter is lacking. Rather than lament about what could have been, take the necessary time to review and revise your query, then get back out there with your second batch.

Should you resubmit your edited query to an agent you really want to work with? Some agents will consider a heavily overhauled query after rejection, but the odds are against you.

Which agents to send queries to first? If you're convinced your query letter is rock solid, why not start with your A list? If you're at all uncertain, or less of a gambler, consider starting with a mix of your A, B, and C-ranked agents. A positive response from any one of them will bolster your confidence, and if the entire batch is rejected, at least you haven't burned through every one of your top picks.

Last, but by no means least, agents earn their income from a percentage of your royalties, typically 15 to 20% of your earnings. They will never charge reading fees or a fee to represent you. If you receive an offer that requests either, run, don't walk, in the other direction (#AR).

Publisher Submissions

The first step is to compile a master list of publishers currently accepting unagented submissions that meet your criteria (genre/sub-genre and word count). Make sure to indicate the estimated size of the press (micro, small, medium, large). This can best be determined by their catalog and the number of authors they represent.

Once again, I'd encourage you to compile a separate list of publishers you've reviewed, but eliminated, with the reason for your decision. Additionally, your master list should include the name of the publisher, main contact, website URL, dates submitted/responded, with a place for additional notes, and a brief note about their guidelines and any open or closed reading periods (it's not unusual for publishers to establish date parameters for submissions).

Unlike agented submissions, independent publishers willing to look at unagented submissions often accept full manuscripts, sometimes using an online portal for uploading. Follow the instructions and wait. In the publishing world, patience is a much-needed virtue.

At this point you might be asking, "Where do I get the names of agents and publishers?" It's a fair question, and there are several ways to find names, starting with a simple internet search for "List of Literary Agents" or "List of Mystery Publishers." There's also Publishers Marketplace (#AR), a good starting place.

Additionally, many associations will maintain a list, some available to the public, and others as a members' only benefit (see The Write Life for more information on associations).

Magazines geared to writers are another good resource, many with online databases. Yet another is querytracker.net, an online search engine that offers free and premium (paid) services (#AR).

Pro Tip: Authors often thank their agent and publisher in their acknowledgments. Check books in your genre for possible names.

And now it really is time to get down to business. It's time to turn the page and look at publishing paths in greater detail.

UNDERSTANDING YOUR OPTIONS

TRADITIONAL (TRADE BOOK) PUBLISHERS

A.K.A. THE BIG FIVE

THESE ARE the publishers most likely to be stocked at brick-and-mortar stores. That's because the Hachette Book Group, HarperCollins, Macmillan Publishers, Penguin Random House, and Simon & Schuster, or "Big Five," as they are collectively known in the biz, control roughly 80% of that market and account for approximately 90% of the titles on bestseller lists. That leaves 20% of the brick-and-mortar market (and 10% of bestseller lists) for independent, hybrid, and self-published authors combined. It's worth mentioning that the odds of self-published books finding space in a physical store are slim to none. If nothing else, these are statistics to remember going forward, if only to keep your expectations realistic.

The bottom line? The Big Five rule the book publishing world, and few unknown writers get past their very stringent gatekeeping. Of those who do, one in five will earn back their royalty advance.

A tough business, to be sure, and it's getting tougher.

There was a time when the "Big Five" were the "Big Six," and, most recently, they almost became the "Big Four."

Mergers and acquisitions have been altering the publishing landscape since the 1990s. They may not seem relevant to you as a writer, but the reality is fewer players erode the dwindling traditional publishing opportunities available for unknown authors.

In August 2022, Stephen King's disapproval over the proposed merger between Penguin Random House (PRH) and his own publisher, Simon & Schuster, led him to voluntarily testify for the U.S. government in an anti-trust trial aiming to stop the $2.18 billion merger. The lawsuit argued that the acquisition would create a publisher with too much influence over books and author payments. The planned merger was blocked by Judge Florence Pan of the United States district court for the District of Columbia on October 31, 2022.

A (DEEPER) DIVE INTO THE BIG FIVE

Each of the Big Five represent smaller publishers who in turn represent dozens more publishing interests, known as imprints. Here's a quick look at the current state of the market (#AR).

HACHETTE BOOK GROUP (HBG): Headquartered in New York City with offices in California, Colorado, Massachusetts, North Carolina, Oregon, Pennsylvania, Tennessee, as well as Hachette Book Group Canada, Inc., a marketing and publicity company based in Toronto, HBG publishes approximately 2,600+ books each year. Publishing groups include Grand Central Publishing, Hachette Audio, Hachette Nashville, Little, Brown and Company, Little, Brown Books for Young Readers, Orbit, Perseus Books, and Workman Publishing. A few dozen imprints fall under each of these groups. HBG works exclusively with literary agents, and will not consider or respond to unsolicited submissions, manuscripts, or queries.

HARPERCOLLINS: Headquartered in New York City, HarperCollins has publishing operations in seventeen countries and more than 120 branded imprints around the world, publishing approximately 10,000 new books every year in 16 languages, with a print and digital catalog of more than 200,000 titles.

MACMILLAN PUBLISHERS (MACMILLAN): A division of the Holtzbrinck Publishing Group, a large family-owned media company headquartered in Stuttgart, Germany, Macmillan is a global trade publishing company operating in more than 70 countries, with imprints in the United States, Germany, the United Kingdom, Australia, South Africa, and India. The company operates eight divisions in the United States: Celadon Books, Farrar, Straus and Giroux, Flatiron Books, Henry Holt and Company, Macmillan Audio, Macmillan Children's Publishing Group, St. Martin's Press, and Tor Publishing Group. None accept or respond to unsolicited manuscripts or queries.

PENGUIN RANDOM HOUSE (PRH): Headquartered in New York City with operations in more than 20 countries across six continents, Penguin Random House is home to about 275 international publishing imprints, annually publishing more than 70,000 digital and 15,000 print titles, with 100,000+ eBooks available worldwide. The PRH website offers advice on getting published, but it's nothing you don't already know. Find an agent. Be patient. Lather, rinse, repeat.

SIMON & SCHUSTER: Founded in 1924, Simon & Schuster is owned by ViacomCBS, which publishes such imprints as Atria, Scribner, and Simon & Schuster. With multiple bestselling authors to their credit, Simon & Schuster does not accept unagented submissions. They do, however, suggest that writers who want to pursue self-publishing check out Archway

Publishing, a subsidiary of Simon & Schuster. Proceed with caution: Archway is outsourced to Author Solutions, a vanity press with several imprints.

DREAMING THE DREAM

Despite the almost insurmountable odds, thousands of aspiring authors share the dream. But dreaming isn't going to grab a top-notch agent's attention, and that's exactly what you'll need to land a Big Five contract. Beyond a fresh concept and killer manuscript, you'll need a combination of luck (right place, right time), dogged determination, and months, if not years, of concerted effort.

LUCK: My mother always told me, "The harder you work, the luckier you get." She wasn't right about everything, but she was right about that.

A FRESH CONCEPT: Not as easy as it sounds. To quote Mark Twain, "There is no such thing as a new idea. It is impossible. We simply take a lot of old ideas and put them into a sort of mental kaleidoscope. We give them a turn and they make new and curious combinations. We keep on turning and making new combinations indefinitely; but they are the same old pieces of colored glass that have been in use through all the ages." Twain aside, if you write with the view of cashing in on this year's hottest trend, remember that those books would have been acquired two to three years earlier. Chances are that market is already saturated, and the trend has started to spiral downward. (How many people thought they could write the next *Twilight* or *50 Shades of Grey?*)

DOGGED DETERMINATION: It's hard enough to land an agent, and not all agents are created equal. You want someone who can submit to and get an audience with a trad publisher. Publishing houses only work with agented authors, and those agents tend to be people they know and trust. Polish your manuscript, synopsis, and query letter until they shine, make your list of agents as recommended in Getting Down to Business, and start pitching with this in mind.

CONCERTED EFFORT: Kathryn Stockett spent five years writing *The Help*. It took another three years, numerous revisions, and a whopping 60 rejections before she landed an agent. That's a concerted effort. Writing your first draft during NaNoWriMo and sending it to ten agents on December 1st is not.

TIMELINES

The best agents will use their expertise to suggest edits to your manuscript and proposal *before* approaching publishers. This process takes time and there is no guarantee that your manuscript will be picked up by a publishing house. Even in the best-case scenario, submissions seldom lead to an offer right away. Manuscripts can take months, sometimes years, to find a publisher.

Let's say you are one of the lucky chosen few. Average advances (a royalty paid based on projected sales) for a new, unknown author vary widely. But with a traditional publisher you can optimistically expect an amount starting in the low thousands, and quite possibly more. Of course, a new author with name recognition (celebrities, sports legends, etc.) will earn upwards of $250,000, which might seem unfair unless you weigh the percentage (rather than the dollar amount) of financial risk taken by the publisher. I've gone into more detail on advances, royalties, and royalty structure in Money Matters.

Once the deal is sealed the publisher takes over, controlling and financing every step of the publishing process. This includes everything from editing and book design to distribution and promotion. I use the word controlling, instead of managing, because that is the reality. Expect to relinquish all rights: hardcover, trade paperback, mass market, digital, audio, foreign, film, etc. The characters you've created, the fictional world they might live in, will all belong to the publisher. Even a short story featuring your protagonist cannot be published elsewhere without their permission. In other words, the trad publisher literally controls the narrative, not only because they've paid you well for the privilege, but because they have a team of experts who are skilled at doing so. If you're the sort of person who needs frequent updates, wants to take an active role, or expects to approve every editorial change, a trad publisher is the wrong dance partner.

EXCEPTIONS TO THE RULE

While it's true that traditional publishing houses don't accept unagented submissions, some imprints or divisions within imprints might. The only way to find out is to check out the website for every imprint under a Big Five umbrella and start digging. Even if your search yields a potential publisher, you're still going to need patience. There may be periods when they are closed for submissions or limited-time mentorship programs for debut or underrepresented voices. Response times may be lengthy. Some may only respond if they are interested, and that interest could take upwards of a year—they're not in a rush to make your dreams come true.

As is the case with independent publishers, not all imprints make it for the long haul. You may or may not have heard of Random House's digital imprints Hydra (sci-fi, fantasy, horror) and Alibi (mystery/thriller), or their romance/women's fiction lines, Loveswept and Flirt. That's because they only lasted a few years before they were closed. Other imprints that may once have accepted unagented submissions, such as Macmillan's Farrar, Straus and Giroux, discontinued the practice because of the sheer volume of unsolicited manuscripts, proposals and query letters received daily.

But all is not lost. Heartdrum, an imprint of HarperCollins, self-described as a "Native-focused imprint of HarperCollins Children's Books," is open to submissions from unagented Native writers. Yen Press, a publisher of graphic novels, which Hachette co-owns with Kadokawa Corporation, does (or did at the time of publication) accept unagented queries. They also actively seek qualified Japanese and Korean translators for their Manga, Manhwa, and Light Novel books. Also under the HarperCollins umbrella is the Write for Harlequin website (#AR).

No Deal Doesn't Mean No Hope

By now you've accepted the reality that most unknown authors won't land a Big Five publishing contract, but that doesn't mean your book can't find a good home, and it doesn't mean your only option is to self-publish. There are many reputable independent publishers who offer traditional publishing paths on a smaller scale. Most don't require an agent. We'll take an in-depth look at your options, from micro to large press, next.

INDEPENDENT PUBLISHERS
MICRO, SMALL, MEDIUM, AND LARGE

LET'S FACE IT. Landing a deal from one of the few remaining traditional publishing houses is a bit like winning the lottery. You might get lucky, but odds are you'll play the same numbers for a decade and never win much more than a free ticket. Yet for many writers, true validation will only be achieved by signing a traditional publishing contract. The self-, hybrid-, or social-publishing routes are not for them. Somehow, those other options don't seem "worthy." It could be they just want their work to be considered, no matter how remote the chance, for an award or newspaper review from which self-published authors are still often excluded. Or maybe they just want to avoid the self-publishing stigma that still exists in many circles.

I get it. You want to be part of the club. I was one of those writers myself and I'm not ashamed to admit it. After all, knowing a publisher believes in you, and in your words? That's powerful stuff. And if my first indie publisher hadn't believed in me back in 2014, I honestly don't know where I'd be today. Maybe in the same place. Maybe not. I do know I will be forever grateful for how I got my start, even if "The End" wasn't exactly how I'd envisioned it.

Which brings me to the "independent" publisher, a segment of the book publishing market that has grown in leaps and bounds as Print on Demand (POD) has become not only more accessible, but the norm. Furthermore, independent publishers play an important and powerful role in today's publishing landscape.

Before we get too far ahead of ourselves, let's define the term "independent publisher" which, ironically, is not the same as "independently published." And, yes, I know what you're thinking: whoever coined these terms (along with "hybrid author" and "hybrid publisher") should have purchased a thesaurus. Alas, it's too late now.

So, back to our definitions, such as they are. An *independently published author* (also known as an "indie" author) is a fancy way of saying self-published. An *independent publisher* is independently owned and managed, not part of any larger publishing house and in no way associated with any of their smaller imprints.

But defining an indie publisher doesn't stop there, because if there's ever a case to be made for "one size does not fit (or in this case, define) all," this is it. You're about to learn the differences, from micro to large independent. But before we go there, a few words of caution: reputable publishers, no matter their size, never advertise looking for authors. With rare (and I do mean *rare*) exceptions, they will never contact you out of the blue, and certainly not with an ironclad offer of representation.

Sadly, there are any number of scams and scammers out there that have no hesitation in luring unsuspecting authors into their net (#AR). Before you sign with *any* independent publisher, research them online and get answers to these important questions:

- What sort of gatekeeping do they employ with submissions? This doesn't have to mean agented, but there should be a review process of some kind. If everyone who submits gets accepted, you are dealing with a vanity press, *not* an independent publisher.
- Is the website professionally designed and frequently updated? Does it promote authors and their books, or is the focus on promoting the press and what they can do for authors? The first is a positive, the second a warning sign.
- How long has the company been in business? Who are the owners and/or staff members and what are their credentials? A well-intentioned mission statement isn't enough. For an example, read "Whatever Happened to Catstone Books?" on the Writer Beware website (#AR).
- Have any complaints been registered on sites such as Writer Beware? What about comments on Querytracker.net? Online in general? Here again, the internet is your friend.
- How many authors does the press represent? It never hurts to contact individual authors for their feedback. In my experience, most authors are upfront in this regard. Even those who are more cautious speak volumes if they decline to comment.
- How many books are in their catalog? None yet? Then tread with extreme caution. A handful? Are they older or recent releases? How often do they publish? Extended gaps in production may be an indicator of past or present financial difficulty. Select a handful of titles and check their reviews, rankings, and ratings on Amazon. Read the "look inside the book" excerpts to see what the editing is like and get a

sense of the quality of the material. I always check Goodreads as well.

- Where are the books being distributed? Do they publish on retailers outside of Amazon (Barnes & Noble, Apple Books, Kobo, etc.)? If it's Amazon only, move on. You can do that yourself for half the cost and probably twice as well.
- Has the publisher been vetted by a writing association? For example, Mystery Writers of America has an Approved Publisher List (#AR), which requires a publisher to uphold professional standards of good business practice and fair treatment of their authors. NOTE: In this section, I'll be referring to contracts and royalty structures. Money Matters explains both in detail. Feel free to skip ahead and come back when you're ready.

Back already? Okay then, let's look at the options:

MICRO PRESS

A micro press is typically a one- or two-person operation, often started as a way of self-publishing their own work(s). As a rule, there are no paid employees, which can mean:

- Editing, proofreading, interior page design, cover art, and accounting (preparation and payment of royalty statements) will either be done in-house by the principal(s) (owners) or farmed out on a work-for-hire basis.
- Quality and delivery of published materials will vary widely.
- Promotional support and budget will be minimal to non-existent.

- An advance on future royalties is unlikely.
- No Advance Reader Copies (ARCs).

Self-publishing takes hard work, commitment, business acumen, and a certain amount of cash flow. Operating a micro press increases those needs tenfold. While some micro publishers may "grow up" to become small presses, most, like the ill-fated mom-and-pop diner competing with the big money of restaurant chains, will fail within the first year. Eighty percent will shutter their doors within five. Because of that, you will want to ensure that any contract you sign has a straightforward, fair, and clearly defined reversion of rights clause in the event of insolvency or closing of the business. Even with that, know that the odds of recouping any royalties owed to you are remote if the micro press does close. Legal action is expensive, and chances are there would be no money in the coffers to pay you regardless.

Since the value-add of signing with a micro press is limited (truthfully nothing more than you can do yourself with a modicum of effort), your share of royalties earned should reflect that, e.g., an equal 50/50 split between publisher and author on net royalties for print and e-book. Additionally, do not give up any publishing rights where there is no reasonable expectation of the micro press following through, such as film, foreign, mass market, hardcover, or audiobook rights. You may be able to sell those rights elsewhere.

Warning: if you are asked to contribute towards any of the costs of production (as outlined in the first bullet point), you're not dealing with a micro publisher, but a hybrid publisher and possibly a vanity press.

The same holds true for marketing. Regardless of publication path, the bulk of advertising and promotion will undoubtedly fall on you, the author. This will be even more evident with a micro press who, by their very nature, are not flush with cash or marketing savvy. That said, advertising and promotional options should *never* be payable to the publisher from a fee-for-service menu, but rather to an independent and completely unrelated third party, e.g., social media ads, bookmarks, etc.

One final caveat: be watchful of contracts that require a bulk purchase of your books. POD publishers (which all micro presses use) can print as few as one copy of your book, or as many as you desire. At a bare minimum you should receive one free author copy in all digital formats, as well as print. Lastly, author copies, if you wish to order some for friends, family, or a book launch, should be discounted to 50% off the list price (plus shipping and tax). The press won't make money on those, but they won't lose money either. And isn't that what partnerships are supposed to be about?

Have I scared you off micro publishers yet? While it might seem that way, my intent is to apprise you of the potential pitfalls, of which there are many. But there are solid micro presses out there, too. My own imprint, Superior Shores Press, which I use to self-publish my books, also qualifies as a micro publisher for the multi-author Superior Shores Anthologies of mystery and suspense. Did the contributing authors take a chance on me, especially those who were featured in the first multi-author collection, *The Best Laid Plans: 21 Stories of Mystery & Suspense?* Without question.

To be fair, I paid the authors a flat fee per story, was transparent about the process, and had a solid reputation as an author adept at promotion. That said, solid or not (just like so many well-intentioned and passionate micro presses) I *am* and remain (by choice) a one-woman band. If I cease to publish, whether through death or desire, the music will simply stop playing.

Would I consider publishing books by individual authors? Not a chance. The anthologies were a labor of love. Publishing other authors? That's a full-time business, and burnout or disillusionment, probably within a couple of years, is virtually guaranteed.

Whether you choose to sign with a micro press is a decision only you can make. Like any business, they can grow, and you might be getting in on the ground floor of the next big thing. And just like the stock market, where early investors often reap the greatest rewards, every successful independent press had to start somewhere.

SMALL PRESS

Many of the cautions mentioned under micro press also apply to small press publishers, albeit to a lesser extent. Their roster of authors will be greater, the length of time in business longer. Even so, a massive author list, which may seem impressive, can also mean the publisher isn't very selective and/or is trying to grow the business too quickly. The latter isn't a factor if the press has the financial resources and staff to support and manage the growth.

How do you know if a small press is adequately funded and staffed? Checking the "About Us" section is a start, but the truth is there's probably no real way for you to find out beyond taking the precautionary steps we've already talked about.

Once you've done your research and feel adequately reassured, it's time to focus on the benefits of a small press, not the least of which is providing opportunities for unagented authors seeking traditional publication. That's not to say that small presses won't accept agented submissions. Some will, some won't.

In addition to providing all the services outlined in the first bullet point, a small press should provide digital ARCs (print ARCs are unlikely) at least four months prior to the release date, though it may be up to you to find reviewers to send copies to. That said, some small presses will ask their other authors to "blurb" an upcoming release (praise for a book included inside or on the cover).

The time from your book's acceptance to publication varies but is almost always less than that of a larger press, and often less than a year. This is both good and bad. Good in that you aren't waiting in the wings wondering if your book will sell. Bad, because a tight timeline can mean less time to get reviews. It can also mean a rushed editing and proofreading process. Long production times don't necessarily equal improved quality, but any deadline of six months or less, and something is going to give. If that's what you're being offered, question the publication process before signing.

A small press should also share a galley proof (a preliminary, formatted version of your soon-to-be-published novel). Galley proofs are meant for the author, editor, and proofreader to review a book on a chapter-by-chapter basis, and either approve or suggest changes. I've been previously published by two small presses. One required me to participate in the galley proof review. The other did not allow their authors the opportunity to collaborate, preferring to fast track the editing and proofreading process, often with less than desirable results. Suffice it to say I would never again agree to be excluded from the galley proof process, and nor should you. After all, it's your name on the cover. You should have a say in the final product.

When it comes to advertising and promotion, a small press offers minimal support—even though they stand to benefit from every dollar you as the author invests independently towards an ad campaign, a fact that I'll readily admit annoyed me when I was a published by a small press; surely if they reap the royalty rewards, they should contribute their fair share? Not so, I'm afraid, though maybe such a policy will one day become an industry standard.

It's not all doom and gloom, however. Small press publishers worth their salt will hold book sales (where titles in their catalog are discounted for a limited period) one or more times each year. These sales are typically based around the publisher's anniversary or another special occasion or holiday. When accompanied with publisher-prepared artwork, these book sales are an easy way for authors to promote their work on social media with a new hook at no cost (beyond reduced royalties on discounted sales).

Which brings us to royalties.

Small press publishers typically pay royalties based on net receipts (also known as net sales). Based on one of this reporting format, royalties should be in the 30 to 50% range, reported and paid on a quarterly or semi-annual basis, with an expectation of lower royalties for print, and higher for digital.

Medium Press

The closest thing to a large independent, the medium press publisher tends to favor agented submissions, though there are ways for an unagented author to find another way into the fold.

One of the best ways is to have a prior business relationship, and by that I don't mean a novel, but rather a short story or stories included in anthologies published by the press. Many medium presses publish multi-author collections, either for their own imprint, or on behalf of a conference, convention, or charitable initiative. For example, Bouchercon, an annual mystery convention, releases a multi-author anthology in conjunction with their event, as does Malice Domestic, another annual mystery convention. Both anthologies are published by independent presses. (More on Conferences and Conventions in The Write Life.)

Another "in" is to have written exactly what their submission wish list is currently looking for. If that's the case, you'll want to ensure your query letter drives that point home. You'll also want to include a brief, but solid, marketing plan, and any other information which will tell them you're the real deal. Refer to Query Letters in Getting Down to Business.

Medium press independents typically pay royalties in the same way as their small press counterparts, on net receipts with the percentage (royalty rate) paid varying by publisher and often by author. In general, the larger the press, the stronger the sales and marketing support, the higher the advance, and the more units (books) you will sell. With that comes the likelihood of a lower royalty rate than you might receive from a smaller press.

LARGE INDEPENDENT

The closest thing to a contract with a traditional "big five" publishing house, most large independent publishers accept unagented submissions, though agented submissions will always take preference. Getting a referral from one of their published authors, while helpful with any publisher you approach, is especially valuable when the stakes are higher. It might even move your submission up from the slush pile to the "soon to be read" pile.

There is also a harsh reality (don't shoot the messenger): the larger the press, the more submissions they are likely to receive from other hopefuls—hundreds, if not thousands, every year.

Let's be conservative and guess that's one submission a day. Even the largest of the large independents can't publish 365 titles in a year. Because of that (and not necessarily because of the quality of your submission) the odds of rejection intensify tenfold. Most will take it one step further, adding a disclaimer on their website. Here are a couple of actual examples:

> "We receive hundreds of submissions each year, please allow six months for a response. If you do not receive a response within six months, you can assume that the submission has been rejected. Please no phone calls or follow up emails."

"Please allow at least three months for a response. Please do not call our office. If you do not hear back, assume your project doesn't fit our current editorial needs."

In other words, don't call us, we'll call you. Maybe.

Discouraging? It can be. But understanding the business is the first step in setting you apart from the rest.

HYBRID/ASSISTED PUBLISHING

I KNOW several authors who had their pick of publishing path options and chose to go the assisted publishing route. One was even shortlisted for a prestigious "Best Unpublished" manuscript award. She has since gone on to win (and be shortlisted) for numerous North American awards for her hybrid-published historical novel. Another is a well-known book reviewer with a hefty number of "industry in's," should he have elected to play that card. Last, but by no means least, is a talented author I met at a library event when I was first starting out. He believed in his book but accepted that wanting a fast track to publication, along with the demands of a growing family and a full-time job, would eliminate the possibility of traditional paths or self-publishing.

For each of these authors, going this route was *their* best path to publication...with one caveat. They all did their due diligence before signing with a hybrid publisher.

The Award Winner mentioned above compiled a list of her own expectations and determined her "top pick." She then reached out to a handful of authors who had used their services and asked for the unvarnished truth. It helped that, in addition to reading their books, she'd developed a relationship with these authors through writing associations and social media connections. There's no reason you can't apply the same strategy.

The Reviewer routinely receives hundreds of books every year, in the hope that he will write a favorable review. He made a note of every publisher, doing his own homework. He knew he wanted to self-publish. He also knew he didn't want to do the grunt work. One hybrid publisher stood out for consistent quality, and that's the one he selected for his own debut novel.

What all three authors knew, and what I can't stress enough, is the need to proceed with extreme caution. For every legitimate hybrid publisher out there, there are more with the wrong intentions and a polished website. An easy "yes" should never be your benchmark. Trust your intuition when it comes to red flags and, if unsure, ask. There are plenty of forums, including social media, where you can check in with other writers if something seems too good to be true (we talked about that, remember?). And that brings us to the vanity press.

VANITY PRESS A.K.A. THE DREAM STEALERS

Here's a heads up: Vanity press publishers often *look* legitimate, with slick websites and promises of TV and radio ads, social media prowess, bogus testimonials, and so much more. Sometimes they even look more legit than legit publishers. Regardless of their online persona, they will never use the term "vanity" to describe their services, though they will use the term "hybrid publisher" liberally, which can entice the unwitting and uninformed.

Sadly, the claims of a vanity press will be greatly exaggerated and, in most cases, outright fabrications. Their desire to part you from your hard-earned money without any thought or care for you as the author, all while doing virtually nothing to earn their exorbitant fees, is the stuff of legends—in the worst way. That's why I call vanity press operators dream stealers. Because that's exactly what they're doing. Stealing your dreams.

Do *not* let them steal yours.

FINDING THE REAL DEAL

How will you differentiate between a vanity press and a legitimate hybrid publisher?

A legitimate hybrid publisher offers the five fundamentals of trade publishing and self-publishing: editing, proofreading, book design, cover art, and uploading to retail, while adhering to the same industry standards and attention to quality as their traditional counterparts.

While there are ethical and reputable hybrid publishers, there are more bad actors in this arena than well-intentioned companies. Doing your research cannot be overstated!

Even those that mean well might charge premium prices for the services provided, well above the cost you would incur with self-publishing. Let's take book distribution as an example. If you opt to self-publish, you will be responsible for uploading your book to the various retailers, such as Amazon (KDP), Barnes & Noble (Nook), Rakuten KOBO (Kobo), etc., or through an aggregator like Draft2Digital. There's no charge to do this, beyond the time you invest in the process.

But time is money, and it would be unrealistic to expect free book distribution under a hybrid publishing model. Some offer fee-based book distribution packages. Others include book distribution as part of their overall publishing package but make no mistake: included does not mean free. The same can be said for every service provided, from editing to book design and beyond. It's a bit like hiring a professional renovator. The renovator supplies the materials needed—drywall, two-by-fours, paint, etc.—but there will be a markup on the materials, as well as a cost per hour to do the work.

The bottom line? Carefully vetted, hybrid/assisted publishing can be a viable, albeit more expensive, option for those who want greater control of their publishing path without doing all the heavy lifting. That said, there are no guarantees that you will earn back your investment, and few authors will. This isn't a reflection on the hybrid publisher model, either; even traditional publishers lose money on four out of five authors signed. That's just the nature of the business.

FINDING THE RIGHT HYBRID FIT

Let's start by stating two facts: no matter how it's presented, this isn't a partnership—it's a business arrangement. They are the business. You are the client. They are *assisting* you in your path to publication.

It's important to differentiate between a hybrid publisher and a print on demand (POD) publisher. The latter does not offer in-house editorial services before sending it out into the world, they are simply the conduit to publishing your pre-formatted manuscript to retail in print and/or e-book format. For more on POD publishers, see the Self-publishing section.

When searching for a hybrid publisher, start with the Independent Book Publishers Association's (IBPA's) *Hybrid Publisher Criteria*, available for free download (#AR).

The Association's first point, that a hybrid publisher must "define a mission and vision for its publishing program," while important, should not be relied on too heavily. After all, even the worst vanity presses (or perhaps, especially the worst) offer this, often quite convincingly.

Here are a few other areas worth consideration:

TRANSPARENCY: From the editing and design to retail uploads and royalty payments, the publisher's website should be transparent about cost and services offered. Ideally, there will be a sample contract online or made available upon request. (Contract terms and review options are covered in Money Matters.)

REPUTATION: By reputation, I don't mean online testimonials. While some may be legit, they can easily be faked and, let's face it, no company is going to post negative reviews on their website. Instead, visit sites that expose fraudulent publishers and/or rate legitimate ones. Two excellent resources are The Alliance of Independent Authors' (ALLi's) *The Best Self-Publishing Services (And the Worst)* and Writer Beware by Victoria Strauss (#AR).

CATALOG: This should be online, broken down by category, and easily accessible. Have you heard of any of their authors in your genre? Does the publisher seem to specialize? If so, does that specialty align with yours? Taking the research one step further, consider selecting a half-dozen or more names and titles in the catalog and checking the Amazon and Goodreads reader reviews and ratings. Don't be put off by the occasional 1-star rating; reading is subjective. I'd even go so far as to suggest disregarding any 1-star rating that doesn't include a review citing the reason for it. Instead, look at the number of ratings (an indicator of sales) and overall average rating (an indicator of quality). Take the time to read the reviews; it's there where you might find reader comments about editing or other quality issues.

MANUSCRIPT EVALUATION: An unbiased review of your novel's strengths and weaknesses prior to accepting your book for publication. The gatekeeping won't be as strict as that of a traditional publisher, but there will be a general commitment to quality. Manuscripts determined to require additional editing will usually be offered alternate options. These may include a referral to onsite editing or an affiliate partner, or a referral to recommended freelance editors. If this happens to you, take a moment or two to wallow, and then be grateful for their candor.

A vanity press would have accepted your not-quite-ready-yet work without question.

PROFESSIONAL EDITING SERVICES: Your options should include developmental, copy, and content editing, as well as proofreading. Some hybrid publishers offer a pay-per-service model. Others offer an all-inclusive publishing package that excludes editing but includes a final proofread. If you've gotten past the gatekeeper stage, a final proofread might be enough. That said, additional coaching or editing services may be suggested, and in some cases required, by the publisher before moving to the publishing stage. Before you dismiss the advice, however difficult it may be to hear, remember this: a vanity press won't care, a legitimate hybrid publisher will. Don't let your ego get in the way of putting your best book forward.

COPYRIGHT: Always remains with the author. Don't confuse copyright with publishing rights, which is what you, the author, assign to a publisher to publish your novel. Refer back to understanding copyright in Getting Down to Business.

DESIGN SERVICES: Professional cover art (e-book and print) and interior book layout. Check out covers from the publisher's online bookstore, paying special attention to those in your genre. Are they innovative and eye-catching? Or uninspired and unremarkable? Note: some hybrid publishers will allow you to supply your own hi-resolution artwork or photography. Don't be afraid to inquire about options if that's something that interests you.

PUBLISHING PROTOCOL: Legit hybrids use their own ISBNs (International Standard Book Number) and imprint(s) for publishing. They will never use "free" ISBNs assigned through any book retailer and there should be no expectation for you to supply your own. I've included more on ISBNs in the Self-publishing section.

RETAIL DISTRIBUTION: The publisher must be able to upload to retail in print and e-book formats. Some publishers have an upload fee per retailer, others have a flat rate. Both are a cash grab since they are going to make a percentage off every book you sell. Before you sign on the dotted line, take the time to see what current retail royalty rates are for each individual bookseller and compare that with what the publisher is offering. You may also be encouraged to purchase book return insurance for print copies. While returns can be expensive (see Understanding Royalties in Money Matters), book return insurance will likely be even more expensive. After all, hybrid publishers are not in the business of losing money.

AUTHOR COPIES: IBPA's *Hybrid Publisher Criteria* says it best: "If an author is asked to subsidize *or* pay for the full cost of print runs, they should own the physical copies outright and should therefore not be required to pay a 'percent off-list price' amount when ordering copies." While IBPA doesn't specifically address Advanced Reader Copies (ARCs), the same rules should apply. Do not hesitate to ask how ARCs and author copies are handled. You have a right to know, and to understand.

ROYALTIES: Must be completely transparent on the publisher's website and clearly defined in your contract. Further, because you are paying for publishing services, royalties should be significantly higher than what you would be paid by a traditional or independent publisher, who incur the cost of editorial, design, production, etc. There should also be an increased royalty rate for any publisher-operated bookstore purchases, though few sales will be generated from this source. More information on royalties can be found under Traditional Publishing and Independent

Publishing in this section, as well as in Understanding Royalties in Money Matters.

SUPPORT: It goes without saying that there will be support before you sign with a publisher (and likely no end to friendly conversation), but what about after the fact? How and who will you contact if you have a question or concern during the publishing process?

While there are many positives to this path, one consistent negative associated with hybrid publishers are the high-pressure sales tactics, especially when it comes to marketing and promotion. You will be told that getting your book noticed will be difficult, and that's true.

You'll also be told you need a targeted marketing campaign— also true, regardless of path—but they will "help" you with a plethora of ways to spend your money. Let's look at some possible examples:

BOOK CATALOG: Your book listed in the publisher's latest catalog, possibly even a coveted cover spot, might sound like a great opportunity, but at what cost? Be wary of hype promising bestseller status or undefined distribution numbers, and *always* ask for statistics. How many digital downloads per month on average? What's the click-through rate on individual titles? How many of those clicks result in a direct sale? How, what, and where are print copies distributed? Those statistics should be available, and you have a right to know the answers.

PRESS RELEASES: A pre-packaged statement about your book and all pertinent details, distributed to relevant newspapers and magazines. It should include anything unique about the story or you as an author as a hook to entice the outlet to include it in their limited space. Sometimes outlets will run the release exactly as-is, and on rare occasions they will contact you for an interview to do an expanded story with a different angle. If picked up for publication, it can be great free exposure to a wide audience. However, there are never any guarantees that a press release—even one you paid for—will get any further than languishing in an editor's inbox. (For more on this, see Money Matters: Advertising and Promotion.)

Video Book Trailers: If you're hopeless with creating videos, this may be a worthwhile investment, but it wouldn't hurt to do some comparison shopping. There are a lot of talented people out there offering comparable, and possibly better, rates. You'll also need to think of how and where you'll promote the book trailer.

Launch Parties: This is another area to do some comparison shopping. Many blog tour companies also specialize in virtual launch parties.

One final caveat: unless you have unlimited funds, most of the advertising and promotion will fall on your shoulders. Make sure you have enough time to successfully market your book, and you're planning ahead to keep track of all the moving pieces.

An assisted publishing route should mean exactly that: assistance with your path to publication. At a minimum, signing with a hybrid publisher should offer an expectation of professional editing and design services, publishing to recognized industry standards, effortless print and digital retail distribution, and higher than industry average royalties. As for the optional add-ons, preparing a cost-benefit analysis of each one is a good place to begin (#AR).

SELF-PUBLISHING

IF YOU ARE an organized individual who wants control over every aspect of your writing journey, from inception to publication to publicity and beyond, self-publishing may be a good option for you. However, if you think self-publishing is a fast, easy, and inexpensive way to get your book to market, think again. Yes, the costs associated with getting your book out there will be considerably less than what you would incur with a hybrid publisher, but that doesn't mean there aren't expenses. Remember, in this role you are no longer the author, you are the **PUBLISHER**, which means accepting financial responsibility as well as complete accountability for the quality of the book. After all, it's your name on the cover and, ultimately, your reputation.

But back to the expenses. At a bare minimum you will have paid for professional editing (do not, I repeat do NOT, skip this step), proofreading (ditto), and, unless you're a gifted graphic artist, cover art. There are also the interior design elements of the manuscript required for retail and wholesale upload. While I encourage you to learn to format your books yourself, you will need to purchase formatting software (#AR). You'll also need a unique ISBN for each format of your book (e-book, hardcover, trade paperback, mass market). (More on formatting and ISBNs will follow later in this section, under BOOK BASICS.)

There's also going to be a learning curve. Not to mention ongoing advertising and promotion. All of that is going to take not just money, but many, many hours of your time.

Will you recoup your investment? According to WordsRated (#AR), a non-commercial, international research data and analytics group, the numbers look like this:

- 300 million self-published books are sold each year.
- The average self-published book sells 250 copies.
- The average self-published author makes $1,000 per year from their books.
- 33% of self-published authors make less than $500 per year.
- 90% of self-published books sell less than 100 copies.
- 20% of self-published authors report making no income from their books.

On the plus side, the same study reports that:

- More than 1,000 self-published authors made $100,000 last year from Amazon.

Of authors who have published their first book in the last 10 years:

- 1,200 traditionally published authors have earned $25,000+ a year.
- 1,600 self-published authors have earned $25,000+ a year.

I'm not trying to talk you out of it. Self-publishing can be a rewarding and personally enriching experience, one that I've embraced and benefitted from. That said, I'm not buying a chateau in France any time soon.

There's also the stigma that still exists when it comes to self-published work. There are some conferences that won't offer panel spots to indie authors. Likewise, some writing awards exclude self-published work. That said, many conferences and awards now treat indie and traditionally published authors with equal respect, and acceptance in the market continues to grow.

Can self-publishing books hit number 1 on Amazon and other retailers? Absolutely, and in multiple categories, though I know firsthand that, bragging rights aside, the achievement is by no means default entry into a celebrity book club endorsement or a movie deal.

Can self-publishing be a stepping stone to movie deals or signing with one of the Big Five? The answer is yes, though fair warning: they are a far cry from an everyday occurrence. Two well-known examples are *Still Alice* by Lisa Genova and *50 Shades of Grey* by E.L. James.

But we're getting ahead of ourselves. Before any of those scenarios can happen, you're going to have to do the work.

BUSINESS BASICS

I've titled this section Business Basics because that's exactly what self-publishing is, a business. *Your* business. While you can list the publisher of your book as your name, e.g., Judy Penz Sheluk, I strongly encourage you to set up a publishing imprint, which adds a layer of professionalism to your product (and yes, your book is a product). For example, my publishing imprint is registered as Judy Penz Sheluk (Sole Proprietor) DBA (doing business as) Superior Shores Press, which is renewable for a fee every five years. On the copyright page of all my books, the publisher is listed as "Superior Shores Press, copyright © (year) Judy Penz Sheluk."

When selecting a name, you'll need to do a search to ensure the name isn't already registered, and it shouldn't be part (or all of) your name, e.g., Judy Penz Sheluk Press. Starting an online search which will help narrow the possibilities, and both Google and Amazon are good entry points for this. But you'll also need to search national trademark name databases to make sure the name you finally decide on isn't legally registered to someone else (#AR). Once you've registered your name, you may want to go the extra mile and have a logo developed, either by the same person you'll hire for your cover art, or a logo designer. (A quick online search will provide plenty of options.)

Because rules and regulations for small business vary by country, as well as state/province, consult with an accountant who can provide guidance with setting up a publishing imprint and provide advice on registration, tax implications and requirements, and acceptable business write-offs. Note I said "guidance with" versus "can set up a" publishing imprint, because it's usually fairly straightforward to register a business. You'll have enough expenses going forward, no point paying an accountant their hourly rate PLUS the business registration fee.

You'll also need to set up a separate bank account with checking privileges, as well as a solid record-keeping system for income and expenses. The latter is something you've probably already thought about, but what you may not have realized is that income tax slips may not be provided for royalty income. The same holds true for grant programs and contest winnings. Despite that, you are required to declare that income at tax time, in the same way you would as a freelance writer or consultant. Of course, your accountant should have already told you that. If they didn't, find another accountant.

Because the United States and Canada have a reciprocal income tax agreement, each U.S.-based retailer will require

Canadian authors to complete a W-8 BEN form (#AR) to certify that your country of residence for tax purposes is in Canada, and that you agree to abide by Canadian tax laws for any royalties earned. In return, you won't have a portion of those royalties withheld to pay U.S. taxes, and you won't need to file a U.S. tax return. Seriously, who wants to pay income tax to two countries?

BOOK BASICS

I've structured this sub-section in the order I'd suggest taking care of things, rather than alphabetically (though it's not a hard and fast rule).

I've covered copyright basics earlier, but to recap: technically, you own the copyright the minute your work exists, which means you are not required to file (and pay a fee) for copyright protection. Personally, I recommend filing the paperwork, at least for novel-length material, if for no other reason than peace of mind, but the decision is yours to make.

You will also need a copyright page which includes your disclaimer, e.g., "This is a work of fiction," copyright year/name, publisher, editor, proofreader, cover artist, edition number, and ISBNs. Easiest way to figure this out? Open a few books, review the disclaimers, and take it from there (#AR).

AUTHOR BIO & PHOTO

Your bio (#AR) should be written in third person, be 100 words or less, no more than two paragraphs, and keep it relevant. Even if your book is science fiction, this is not the time to mention that you're a Trekkie. If you've written a legal thriller and you're a lawyer or a paralegal, that's relevant. You should also have a professional author photo taken to include with your bio.

ISBNs

An International Standard Book Number (ISBN), the barcode at the back of a book, is a unique number assigned to each version of a book. In Canada, ISBNs are free (#AR). In the U.S. ISBNs must be purchased through the Bowker Agency (#AR), the only official source of ISBNs in the United States. Because part of the ISBN coding identifies the publisher of record, traditional, independent, and hybrid publishers should supply the ISBN. Self-published authors will need to obtain (in Canada) or purchase (in the U.S.) ISBNs under the name of their publishing imprint. Note: The International Book Publishers Association (IBPA) offers a member discount on Bowker purchases.

Once you get to the book upload stage, you'll discover that many retailers, including Kindle Direct Publishing, Barnes & Noble Press, and some Print on Demand (POD) services will provide a "free" ISBN. The catch? You can't use that ISBN with any other publisher. You'll also need to list the issuer of the free ISBN as the publisher, and not your publishing imprint. Not exactly sounding free anymore, is it?

Formatting

As an author, you've learned to properly format a manuscript, but readers aren't going to purchase your Word document. They'll be buying your e-book, or a printed paperback or hardcover copy. Because of that, you'll need to have your book formatted before uploading it for sale. There are three ways to do that:

1. Reformat your Word document to meet specific conversion requirements. Kobo Writing Life has an excellent tutorial on how to do this, but writer be

warned: this option is far from simple (#AR). Draft2Digital also offers free formatting, and they will allow you to use the formatted files on other platforms (#AR).

2. Purchase formatting software. Be sure you select one that will allow you to format an unlimited number of books (always think ahead, never restrict your options!) for *multiple* retailers, in print and digital versions. There should be an option to upload sample material or an offer of a free trial period. I stress the word multiple because a "free" formatting option will probably restrict where you can sell your book. Examples of formatting software include Atticus, Vellum, Adobe InDesign, and Scrivener (#AR).

3. Hire a book formatting service. A good option for the tech-averse, though the cost to do this will probably be as much as or more than purchasing your own software, especially if you plan to publish additional books (#AR).

ARCs (Advance Reader Copies)

Unless you have already uploaded your book to retail, you won't be able to supply print ARCs, but once you've formatted your book, you should have digital copies (PDF, EPUB, and MOBI versions) to email to reviewers.

Advance reviews are used for "blurbs" on the back cover and inside as "praise for" (you see this a lot in e-books since they don't have a back cover). You may also choose to include a blurb on the front cover.

Pro Tip: It's okay to take a snippet of a longer review and use it as a blurb.

If you've been networking through writing associations,

conferences, or conventions, you may have an author or two willing to blurb your book. You can also try your local paper, though the reality is fewer and fewer newspapers offer book reviews, and most won't even consider self-published novels. You may have better luck with a small community paper; this is discussed in more detail in Money Matters: Advertising and Promotion.

There are also review sites which charge a fee, such as Kirkus Reviews and Midwest Book Reviews though, in the interest of their reputations, neither can guarantee a positive review (#AR).

Finding "known" authors or experts to blurb your book can be a challenge. Improve your odds by allowing six to eight weeks for the blurb. It's perfectly okay if it's still in the final editing/proofreading stage. Minor mistakes are expected in an ARC. It's even okay if all you have is a temporary placeholder as the cover. Just be sure the cover of your ARC is clearly marked as ADVANCE READER COPY – Uncorrected Author Proof, Not for Resale — and that the same wording is used on the copyright page.

Ideally, you'll have two or three blurbs, but worst-case scenario, you can always publish without any. Don't let a lack of reviews become an excuse to give up.

Cover Art

We're not supposed to judge a book by its cover, but let's face it, we do, and good covers help sell books. Period.

Let's look at the nitty gritty. Print templates are available at no cost from your POD publisher. Each publisher uses a different template and has different rules, but the templates are based on the size of your book, paper, and page count. You will need to include an ISBN. Because you may want to change the retail price of your book in the future, never include the price on the cover.

Ideal e-book covers have a height/width ratio of 1.6:1, with 1,600 x 2,650 pixels as the optimum size, created as a jpeg or TIFF file.

When it comes to cover design, you have two options:

1. Hire a professional graphic artist who specializes in print and e-book covers. Be sure this is treated as work-for-hire and that you own the copyright to the artwork. Some writing associations offer discounts and/or recommendations for this service. Always credit the artist on the copyright page.

2. Do it yourself. Unless you're a graphic artist, this can be tricky. Yes, there are inexpensive online options (Canva comes to mind) which may be helpful for e-book covers, but that won't help you when it comes to POD templates. You can also use free templates from KDP, but that will restrict you to using that cover only on Amazon. In both cases, you will need to own the copyright to any images you use or purchase a license to use them.

Jacket Copy / Retail Blurb / Back of Book Blurb

The sales pitch, also known as the jacket copy, back of the book blurb, or retail blurb, is the one thing you really need to get right, so take your time with it. What is it you want the reader to know? What is it you want to tease? What's the message you want them to take away? Remember, no spoilers (which means you cannot include some clever diddy you wrote in chapter 19). Unlike beta readers, the more input you can get on this, the better, and test-driving different versions can be a fun way to interact with potential readers on social media, all while drumming up interest in your soon-to-be released book.

RETAIL BASICS

DIRECT TO CONSUMER

As a self-published author, you have three main ways of selling your books direct to consumer:

1. ON YOUR WEBSITE: You will need to set up an e-Commerce platform. Unless you're tech-savvy, it will mean hiring someone to manage this for you. You'll also be responsible for delivery, customer service questions (can't open file, package not received, etc.) If you choose to do this, do it in conjunction with one or more of the other online sales options.

2. AT A MARKET, BOOK LAUNCH, LIBRARY EVENT, OR OTHER IN-PERSON VENUE: If you're the outgoing sort who loves to meet and mingle with readers, these can be fun while providing good networking opportunities, but in my experience, they are seldom lucrative.

3. ON CONSIGNMENT: Arts councils, independent bookstores (including used bookstores), and local businesses will often accept books on consignment; some offer "Meet the Author" days. Since margins on print books are slim, and consignment fees range from 20% to 40%, this is not the road to riches, though it can help you gain recognition in your community and, in turn, help to build a loyal following.

AGGREGATORS, RETAILERS & DISTRIBUTORS

You have your final formatted files and cover art and are ready to get your book in the market. You now have two options: put it on pre-order or publish immediately. For established authors or those with lots of advertising cash, pre-orders can be a way to generate buzz for an upcoming book. Big Five publishers in particular use pre-orders very effectively as a marketing tool.

For first-time authors who haven't built up a huge following—or advertising budget—there's no real benefit in holding off. Even readers who are interested in a book often won't pre-order, preferring instead to wait until release date. That said, there's no right or wrong approach, and the length of the pre-order period can be weeks or months, during which time you can upload new files if necessary. Because pre-orders aren't sales, you won't be paid royalties and, apart from a social platform like Goodreads, books cannot be reviewed or rated prior to release.

There are three main avenues to get your book out there. For each option, you will have an opportunity to review your book as it will be seen on the various platforms before approving for sale.

Aggregators

An aggregator is a one-stop online distributor that will list your book with several online booksellers, as well as library and subscription services. An excellent example of this is Draft2Digital (D2D) (#AR), whose digital storefronts (D2D's term for retailers and subscription services) include Amazon, Apple Books, Baker & Taylor, Barnes & Noble, bibliotheca, BorrowBox, Hoopla, Kobo, Overdrive, Palace Marketplace, Scribd, Smashwords, Tolino, and Vivlio.

While D2D may be the easiest option for e-book distribution, at minimum, I'd recommend setting up a direct account with Kindle Direct Publishing (KDP for Amazon), as well as two or more of the more popular e-book retailers in the U.S. and Canada (see Online Retailers, next).

Setting up a Draft2Digital account is free, though you'll need to provide banking information, tax ID, etc. Once you've done that you can upload your book (at no charge) and select the digital storefronts you want them to distribute on your behalf.

Any royalties will be paid directly to D2D by each individual storefront. In turn, D2D will coordinate those reports and submit one combined monthly royalty statement and payment to you. Their cut is approximately 10%. I've covered royalties in some detail in Money Matters.

Additional information can be found on the D2D website, and I've personally found their customer service to be excellent. Another nice feature is their Universal Book Link option through Books2Read (#AR), where you can create (and custom name) one link for multiple storefronts. Here's an example for my Glass Dolphin Mystery Series box set: https://books2read.com/GlassDolphin.

Online Retailers

As with D2D, there is no charge to set up individual accounts or upload book content because the storefronts earn a portion of your royalties. The main e-book retailers (also known as storefronts or digital storefronts) in the U.S. and Canada are: Amazon (KDP), Google Play (Google Play Partner Center), Kobo (Rakuten Kobo), Barnes & Noble (B&N Press), and Apple (iTunes Connect). Each of these retailers have different royalty rates and payment terms, defined on their websites (#AR). There is usually a minimum payment threshold (anywhere from $10 to $50). If it's too overwhelming for you in the beginning, I'd suggest D2D for all but KDP, which also offers a Print on Demand (POD) option.

Print on Demand (POD) Wholesale Distributors

As a self-published author, Print on Demand (POD) wholesale distributors are your only option when it comes to printing and distributing your book. The term "on demand" also means just that. Your book will be listed as available online and in catalogs but will not be printed until one (or more) copies of your book are ordered. Note: a POD publisher only sells direct to qualifying businesses and institutions, such as bookstores, libraries, and other retailers. They do not sell to consumers, though as an account holder you are able to order author copies at a discounted cost.

While D2D has recently included POD publishing to their service offerings, IngramSpark (#AR) is probably the best-known POD publisher for wholesale global distribution of print books to libraries and brick-and-mortar bookstores. Though account set-up is free, there is a charge to upload your book's interior and cover, as well as a cost if you want to revise either after you've uploaded and approved.

Pro Tip: Some associations, like the Independent Book Publishers Association (IBPA), offer a limited number of free IngramSpark codes. I encourage you to check out the member benefits of writing associations you might consider joining before uploading to Ingram.

Although you can use IngramSpark for e-books as well as POD, their longer-than-industry-average payment terms (90 days) and lower royalty rates (40%) make this a less attractive option than D2D or going direct.

While IngramSpark will supply books to Amazon, you can also use KDP's print option for paperback copies to be sold exclusively on Amazon (you would use the same ISBN as you'd use for IngramSpark).

KDP also offers an "Expanded Distribution" option, however many libraries won't order from Amazon, and bookstores are unlikely to order from their competition. Because KDP, Ingram, and D2D all use the same distribution channels, do not use the Expanded Distribution option if you are using another POD distributor.

KEYWORDS & CATEGORIES

Regardless of where you upload your book, you'll be asked for keywords, usually limited to seven words or a certain number of characters. Note that a keyword can also be a phrase, e.g., antiques shop mystery. The idea is to think of words or phrases that will lead readers to your book when doing an online search. An excellent article, *How to Select Keywords for Your Book* can be found on Babelcube.com (#AR).

You will also be required to select categories for your book. Each retailer operates a bit differently, but you'll be asked to pick a primary subject heading and one to three sub-categories. The basis for the subject heading and categories is derived from Book Industry Standards and Communications (BISAC) codes. For example, the primary subject for this book is LANGUAGE ARTS & DISCIPLINES and the sub-categories are LANGUAGE ARTS & DISCIPLINES / Publishers & Publishing Industry (BISAC code LAN-027000) and LANGUAGE ARTS & DISCIPLINES / Writing Authorship (BISAC code LAN-002000) (#AR).

PRICING

Determining a book's price depends on many factors, not least of which are estimated royalties, a figure that will be provided at the time you upload your book and enter price information. But there's more to pricing than how much money you might make, emphasis on the *might*. Overprice your book and you'll limit sales. Underprice, and you risk giving the impression your book isn't very good. It's also worth noting that some vendors (like Amazon), charge a significantly higher vendor fee for e-books priced below $2.99 or above $9.99.

You may want to put your e-book on sale in the future. A discount from $5.99 to $0.99 is much more appealing than $2.99

to $0.99. Start by doing a price comparison of books in your categories on Amazon and find a happy medium. The good news: it's easy to change the price at any time and doesn't require re-publishing.

I've gone into much more detail (including mathematical examples) on book pricing, vendor charges, and sales in Money Matters: Understanding Royalties.

ROYALTY-BASED SERIALIZED PUBLISHING

Wattpad and Inkitt offer select paid publishing options and both platforms are covered in more detail under the Social Publishing section. While there may be other royalty-based options available, at the time of publication Kindle Vella is the most viable (#AR).

A KDP initiative, Kindle Vella was launched in July 2021 and limited to U.S. authors and readers. Stories uploaded to Kindle Vella are meant to be released in a serialized format with 600 to 5,000 words per episode, with new episodes uploaded on a regular, and frequent, basis.

Compensation on Kindle Vella is royalty- and bonus-based (bonuses are based on customer engagement and activity). The first three episodes of all books are free, then readers purchase tokens to access the rest of the Kindle Vella content. More information on the program and Kindle Vella payment structure can be found on the KDP website under *Kindle Vella - Royalties, Reporting, and Payments*. To publish using Kindle Vella, you will need to create a KDP account. While there is no requirement to do so, completed books can also be published as paperback, e-book, hardcover, and audiobook, with some restrictions.

POST-PRODUCTION

You knew it was coming: marketing. While every author,

regardless of publishing path, will need to familiarize themselves with the ins and outs of promotion, as a self-published author 100% of this will fall on your shoulders. I've covered several possibilities in Money Matters: Advertising & Promotion.

In summary, self-publishing isn't free and no matter what you believed before reading this section, you now realize that it's hard work...and not for the faint of heart. Is it the right path for you? Only you can answer that.

SOCIAL PUBLISHING

THERE ARE any number of reasons for wanting to get your words out into the world. Feedback. Growth. Affirmation. Validation. A forum. Social publishing is one way to do that. In short, it's publishing content directly for your readers with little to no gatekeeping and minimal costs, if any.

This does not mean that all social publishing platforms will be a fit for your work. Some, such as Booksie.com, have minimum age requirements and restrict mature (erotic) content. Whichever platform you choose to use, you'll find commonalities between them and, regardless of platform, your success will depend on your ability to grow a following. While traditional publishing is part of a deeply rooted establishment and process, the community-focused social publishing is a newer format, and one that continues to evolve.

It began with the most obvious example, blogs. The wave of blog popularity and direct link to the success of many authors is undeniable, but it was only the beginning. Social publishing has now branched out to websites and mobile apps tailored to sharing and reading all manner of writing, from poetry to essays to fiction. Some are more professional than others, and most don't offer compensation for writers, so if your goal is purely financial this won't appeal to you. But most do have forums and groups to connect with readers and contests, all to help you hone your craft as a writer. What sets it apart from other publishing paths is the direct reader feedback you get.

WEBSITES & BLOG POSTS

No matter how much you want to simplify it—even if all you want to do is write a weekly blog for a handful of followers—at the very least you'll still need a website and a web provider. Fortunately, there are plenty of options (#AR) and, once again, the internet will be your friend when it comes to choosing the best fit for your current needs. That said, you might want to adjust your vision beyond today and consider the possibilities of tomorrow. After all, your future depends on you and the choices you make now.

When it comes to bloggers, much has been made of the success of the late Julie Powell, famously known for her 2002 food blog, the *Julie/Julia Project*. The blog chronicled her year-long journey recreating every one of Julia Child's 524 recipes in *Mastering the Art of French Cooking: Volume I*. According to *The New York Times*, Powell's blog received more than 400,000 page views that year. Three years later, Little, Brown, and Company published *Julie & Julia: 365 Days, 524 Recipes, 1 Tiny Apartment Kitchen* (later retitled *Julie & Julia: My Year of Cooking Dangerously*). In 2009, Nora Ephron's screenplay *Julie & Julia* (based on Powell's memoir and Child's autobiography, *My Life in France*, written with Alex Prud'homme) hit theaters, garnering multiple nominations and awards for Streep and Ephron, and further acclaim for Powell.

It's a wonderful story, the stuff dreams are made of. But it's also important to put things into perspective.

In 2002, blogging was a "shiny new thing" captivating a growing audience, but still very much in its infancy. Fast forward to today, when there are a reported 1.9 billion (and growing) websites worldwide, approximately one-third—or 600 million—with blogs. It's estimated that six million blog posts are published every single day, meaning roughly 2.5 billion each year. That's *a lot* of competition. Not to mention a general feeling of blog fatigue among followers. Where blog subscribers might once have read every word, they're now often skimming the content, if not skipping it altogether.

Don't get me wrong, I'm not trying to discourage you from blogging. I'm just saying that cooking up an idea doesn't mean anyone's going to come sit at your table. Then again, maybe you don't care about the number of followers you gain (or maybe you're just an optimistic sort). In that case, you'll want to define the type of blog you want to create *and* the reason you want to create it.

Maybe your purpose is one of passion, a cause you believe in, with a mission to spread awareness. Or maybe, as a writer looking for agent representation or independent publication, it might be about building your brand and adding content to your website to prove you're the real deal. There's nothing wrong with that, in fact it's an admirable pursuit. Just remember that dedication and a will to succeed may not be enough.

Next, you'll need to decide how many hours you're willing to commit to blogging. That time commitment will be a direct reflection on the frequency—daily, weekly, bi-weekly, monthly—and length of your posts.

While there are varying opinions on the magic number, I'd suggest monthly isn't going to be enough to build a following, and daily can be a grind. It's one reason why many authors have taken to forming multi-author blogs. Not only do they provide fresh voices every day, joining others alleviates the burden of writing daily posts.

Microblogging, a Twitter-like concept that's become trendy, is another option, essentially a brief message along with a photo. Which reminds me. Remember our copyright section? Copyright applies to photographs, too. Make sure you have the right to use whatever you post.

What about posting content like short stories or excerpts from your book-in-progress? Now you're treading into a gray area. As the author, you own copyright, which gives you the legal means to publish them. That said, if you're considering converting your blog into a full-length book eventually, even Julie Powell didn't just compile a list of blog posts and recipes—she wrote a memoir about her entire *Julie/Julia Project* experience. It's also worth keeping in mind that this isn't 2005. Memoirs have become plentiful, and most are a tough sell. Jane Friedman's "Why Your Memoir Won't Sell" serves as a stark reminder of why, and while there are always exceptions, her article is well worth consideration (#AR).

What if you aren't writing a memoir, but a novel? Will excerpts draw readers in? Perhaps. But be wary of how much you post. A Twitter-length snippet on social media is fine, but a chapter or two and agents and publishers will likely consider the work already published and available to the public. As my mother used to say to my teenage self (admittedly in an entirely different context), "Why buy the milk if the cow is free?" In publishing jargon, this translates to "Already published, no paying market."

What if you've had a short story or two published, and the publishing rights have reverted to you? Adding a sampling as a free value-add to your website might demonstrate expertise, or at the very least, publication credits (though you should be sure to list them that way). Posting an unpublished story? Well, now we're back to our cow scenario.

Most importantly, remember that every hour you invest in blogging will be time taken away from your current work-in-progress, or your efforts to get otherwise published. If all you're looking for is validation and feedback, blogging might be enough. But something tells me you purchased this book to do more.

So do more.

Social Storytelling Platforms (#AR)

The social publishing platform provides a forum for your work to be read and critiqued. Is that enough or do you want more? If so, what does "more" mean to you? Financial success? Recognition, awards, and accolades? Maybe it's simply honing your craft in a community of like-minded individuals.

Whatever your objective, there are pros and cons to every publishing platform, and social publishing is no exception. The best advice I can give you is to always read the fine print before publicly sharing your work.

Here we'll look at a few of the more well-known options in more detail, beginning with the one that started it all: Wattpad.

Wattpad

There are several alternatives to Wattpad available today, but that certainly wasn't the case when Canadian co-founders Allen Lau, an entrepreneur, and Ivan Yuen, a computer engineer, launched Wattpad in 2006. A self-defined "social storytelling platform where new voices write and share," Wattpad provides an online portal for writers to upload and share their work with readers. Wattpad currently boasts a community of 93 million users—and counting—who collectively spend 23 billion minutes on Wattpad each month, with stories available in 50 different languages.

It wasn't always that way. In October 2012, *The Lit Platform* offered an insightful interview into Wattpad's backstory (#AR). In the article, Lau admits that early traffic was "depressing" with a few hundred users at best, though he's quick to point out the company's primary focus of mobile e-reading at the time was a challenge before the era of Kindle and smartphones. Materials available on Wattpad were comprised of works available in the public domain (works no longer subject to copyright).

Today's Wattpad catalog goes well beyond the public domain. In addition to creating new stories using the online portal, writers can submit their work to brand-sponsored writing contests under the Wattpad Brand Partnerships initiative, and enter the annual Watty Awards, which offer a variety of categories in multiple languages, though winning is far from a sure thing with an estimated 300,000 writers entering each year. There's also Wattcon, an annual, one-day conference where writers and readers can meet and mingle. As a Wattpad writer you can also monetize your work in one of two ways: Paid Stories and the Creators Program. Both are by invitation only. There is no financial compensation for writers who are not included in either program.

Whether you've written a short story, novella, or novel, content must be posted chapter by chapter, and not as one single file. In fact, Wattpad recommends publishing in a serialized format, with updates two to three times per week. Content can also be edited after uploading.

This publish-as-you-go format allows readers to follow stories, read new chapters as they're made available, and provide feedback while the story is in progress. Wattpad's Story Statistics metrics measure reader engagement in three ways:

- Total Reads (the number of times a story has been read; a single reader can account for multiple reads).
- Unique Readers (the number of individual readers).
- Engaged Readers (unique readers with 5+ minutes of time spent reading your story).

Wattpad's serialized, publish-as-you-go format isn't unique to

Wattpad. As mentioned in the self-publishing section, Kindle Direct Publishing (KDP) offers a similar model under Kindle Vella, although as a self-publishing (vs. social publishing) platform, authors are paid royalties. Additionally, content posted on Kindle Vella cannot be *freely available* elsewhere on the web. Note the wording: not available freely (meaning at no cost) but freely available (meaning accessible). In other words, you can't publish the same content on Wattpad (or anywhere else, including your own website or social platforms) and Kindle Vella.

The question you might be asking is, "is there traditional publishing light at the end of the Wattpad tunnel?" Truthfully, the odds are slim. The most recent statistic I could find referenced 665 million story uploads to Wattpad, representing 70 million writers. That doesn't mean it can't happen. Success stories include *My Life with the Walter Boys* (Sourcebooks, Netflix) by Ali Novak, *White Stag* (Macmillan) by Kara Barbieri, *Follow Me Back* (Sourcebooks) by A.V. Geiger, and *The Kissing Booth* (Penguin Random House, Netflix) by Beth Reekles. Interestingly, all four are Young Adult novels, although perhaps not surprising; the average age of a Wattpad user is 20; 90% are between the ages of 13 and 40.

INKITT

Imitation is the sincerest form of flattery, and the success of Wattpad continues to spawn alternatives. One of the fastest-growing platforms that also offers author's compensation is Inkitt.

Founded in 2014 in Germany, Inkitt is a self-described "reader-powered publisher." Submissions must be written in English, German, or French, with copyright belonging to the submitting author and, at least at the present time, categorized as fiction. A short story submission video provides an easy-to-follow tutorial for those unfamiliar with the platform.

Content (short story, novel-in-progress, or complete novel)

must meet a stringent set of community and writer's guidelines. Only after a story passes this quality assurance—a process that takes about 48 hours—will it be published onto the Inkitt platform. As with Wattpad, writers are allowed to revise and edit their work. The site also offers monthly contests, a blog which includes writing advice, and community groups.

Writers are also privy to the following:

- Chapter Reads (when a reader starts or continues a story).
- Collected Data (a bar showing how much data has been collected).
- Reviews (reader feedback).
- Demographics graphs (by age, gender, country, where provided by reader).
- Binge rate (the percentage of readers who immediately continue to the next chapter).

Inkitt's algorithm analytics also measures more than 1,200 reader behaviors. Books considered to have bestselling potential are offered a publishing contract with Inkitt's sister app, GALATEA. These authors are provided with cover design, professional editing, royalties, and a marketing team to promote their story.

According to the website, GALATEA has active readers binging over 40 million chapters per month. A section titled *Success Stories* lists *The Millennium Wolves* by Sapir A. Englard, first published in October 2018. Described as an erotic werewolf fantasy, *The Millennium Wolves* passed the one-million-dollar sales mark within ten months of publication, and five million in sales within the first two years. There are now 15 books in the series, all of which have been translated into multiple languages.

While GALATEA is one potential option, it's not an obligation. Because Inkitt authors retain 100% of their rights, they are free to publish their stories on other platforms concurrently, or sign publishing contracts outside of Inkitt.

What are the odds? While Inkitt's user base is a fraction of Wattpad's 93 million (at last check, the Inkitt number was listed as "more than two million readers and writers"), there is still potential to build a strong fan base. Who knows? You might even find a smaller playing field allows you to stand out from the crowd. How you leverage that fan base is up to you.

GOING BEYOND SOCIAL

There are, of course, other social publishing alternatives to blogs, Wattpad, and Inkitt. Much like defining comparables for your book, understanding these three business models can serve as comparables as you delve deeper into the social publishing arena. Remember: due diligence!

But select success stories aside (because we know they are the exception, rather than the rule—even if we dare to hope otherwise), can social publishing hurt or help the average writer? I posed the question to one of my writing association groups. Here's what these authors had to say:

> "My romance books were very successful on Wattpad. Based on those statistics, I queried a mystery series with romantic overtones. The series was picked up by an independent publisher, however, the contract required that the mystery series be written under a name not used on Wattpad."

> "I received a traditional publishing contract, but not for the work posted on Wattpad. The terms of the contract included removing all their work from Wattpad and any other online platform, including blogs."

"Speaking just for the St. Martin's unpublished mystery novel contest (#AR):

1. The excerpt/story posted is no more than 10% of the novel's wordage;

2. The story/excerpt is not for sale in any manner whatsoever, and;

3. That it is the ONLY appearance of part of the novel in any publicly accessible format."

"My opinion is that regardless of where the story was posted, the work would be considered previously published."

"Every publisher (or competition) has different rules regarding previously published work. However, there are often rules that specify that you can post a small excerpt somewhere, not for sale."

"Some publishers will say that posting on a platform like Wattpad is a no-go, but a personal blog is fine, providing that blog has fewer than a certain number of page views a month.'"

"I would suggest that an author should err on the side of caution. If the writer is seeking traditional publication, then don't post that particular story, or an excerpt (beyond snippet length) of a novel you want to pitch, on ANY site."

My personal takeaway from the comments is that if you've established a fan base, those statistics might be meaningful in a query letter. Just don't expect that "already widely read for free novel" you toiled over to generate a book deal.

MONEY MATTERS

CONTRACTS

I'VE SIGNED a few publishing contracts in my time, but I'm not a lawyer, and I'm far from an expert in contract law. What I do know is that the terms of your publishing agreement will determine the *control you retain over your work* for the duration of the contract, however long that might be. Some contracts are two years, others three, five, or seven. There is no "standard." Most contracts (though not all) will automatically renew on an annual basis unless the author requests termination in writing. The contract will also include a clause ("reversion of rights") in the event of publisher bankruptcy or insolvency.

So, what does "control you retain over your work" mean? In a nutshell, these are the rights you will keep (known as the "publishing rights granted") for trade paperback, mass market, hardcover, audio, film, and foreign distribution, etc. of your book. Pay special heed to this section. Before you sign away publishing rights for film, find out if the publisher has ever optioned a book for film. If not, then why would you allow them to control (own) the film rights? This, then, is a publishing right you would (and should) retain control over. Don't be afraid to negotiate.

The contract will also dictate how much and when you'll be paid (e.g., 50% of net sales, quarterly), including any advance on future royalties.

A contract inevitably favors the party who initiates it (publishing is a business, after all). Don't let your desire for representation intimidate or sway you. If something feels wrong or "off," you are well within your rights to question it before signing on the dotted line, and reputable agents and publishers will always allow you time to seek advice. This is because publishing contracts should be a two-way street, open to reasonable (emphasis on reasonable) negotiation on *both* sides, without fear of reprisal. Once you've signed, however, there are no do-overs. Your novel will be subject to the terms, timeline, and conditions set forth in writing. When you get to the contract stage, proceed with equal measures of optimism and caution.

Because of the complexity of contract law, this section is only an introduction to sources listed below that are better equipped to answer any questions you may have. These sites have been listed in alphabetical order, not in any order of preference (#AR).

ALLIANCE OF INDEPENDENT AUTHORS (ALLi)

A non-profit professional association for authors who self-publish, ALLi offers members downloadable templates and annotated contracts, including publisher, ghostwriting, author and/or artist partnership agreements, and reversion of rights. At the time of publication, ALLi is not offering literary agent/author templates. However, in addition to other member benefits, ALLi offers general legal and business advice, as well as free contract review, which includes literary agent/author contracts.

If you're not a member (and even if you are), ALLi's *Understanding and Negotiating Book Publishing Contracts* is a good resource (#AR).

Independent Book Publishers Association (IBPA)

IBPA offers two members-only resources regarding contracts. The first, *A GUIDE TO THE BOOK PUBLISHING AGREEMENT* (#AR) is a seventeen-page sample author/publisher contract listing forty-two distinct clauses, which are broken down into nine sub-sections. Each numbered clause contains the language typically used in a standard publishing contract, along with a detailed definition of the clause. It's a great way to further your understanding of the elements of a contract—you can never be too familiar with the vernacular.

The second is an online discussion forum. Under the broader umbrella of Publishing Law on the website, members can search for previously posted contract advice, or start a new thread with questions or helpful insights.

For non-members and members alike, IBPA's *Hybrid Publisher Criteria* (#AR) includes eleven key elements required to be categorized as a hybrid (versus vanity press) publisher, along with additional points to consider. Available online and in a five-page downloadable PDF, the data contained within it can provide food for thought should you decide to ink a deal with a hybrid publisher.

The Authors Guild

With more than 12,000 members, the Authors Guild is the oldest and largest professional association for writers in North America. It's important to note, however, that there are strict eligibility requirements for joining (#AR).

In terms of publishing contracts, members are provided access to a legal team who will review a contract line by line at no charge to help authors understand what they are getting—and giving away—before signing. Comprehensive written reviews include traditional publishing, e-publishing and self-publishing, agency agreements, multi-media and film options, and freelance agreements.

Both members and non-members can access the Authors Guild's *Model Trade Book Contract* (#AR) which emphasizes fair practice and provides detailed commentary in thirty-five subsections. You might not consider such things as the possibility of publisher insolvency or termination of an agreement, but the Authors Guild has it covered, along with a breakdown of more pleasant topics, like royalties and advances. There is also a similar model contract for Literary Translation Rights. Both are backed by two webinar videos (roughly an hour each), available to the public. Last, but not least, there's an op-ed article regarding morals clauses in contracts.

Reasonable Expectations

Timelines for free contract reviews vary, but a good rule of thumb is a turnaround of ten business days. In other words, don't join the day you get a contract offer and expect to get a contract review the next day. As keen as you might be to receive an answer and get signing, it's unlikely you'll be the only one on any association's list. If timing is of the essence, hiring a lawyer who specializes in literary contract law may be another option, though again, you might not be first on their docket.

Whatever path you choose, and however long the feedback takes, remember: it's okay to ask questions, okay to negotiate in good faith, and okay to protect as many publishing rights as you can. If your publisher has never brokered a single foreign rights language deal, why would you agree to transfer those rights to them? From personal experience I can say that opportunity comes in many forms, and you never know who might come knocking on your door down the road.

The offer of a publishing contract is exciting, but now is the time to think with your head and not your heart. Embrace the possibilities, absolutely, but pay attention to the warning signs, and weigh every single pro and con. Only then will you be able to make an informed decision. I've said it before, and I'll say it again. Publishing is a business, not just "theirs," whoever "they" might be, but yours too. And your business is every bit as important as theirs.

UNDERSTANDING ROYALTIES

Before we get started, there are a few things you need to know as an author: agent, publisher, wholesaler, aggregator, and digital storefronts—everyone, and I do mean everyone, gets a piece of your royalty pie. Here's how it works (and don't stress if it seems confusing. I've included examples later in this chapter):

Digital storefronts & wholesale POD distributors

All sales distribution channels report royalties to the publisher on a monthly basis. This is known as the royalty period. The royalty report will include all book sales from that period, e.g., a March royalty report would include the royalty period of March 1 to March 31.

A percentage (anywhere between 30 to 70%) is deducted from each reported sale as the distributor's share.

Payment to the publisher (Publisher Compensation) for the royalty period is made once per month (provided monetary thresholds are met) and range from approximately 30 to 90 days after the date of sale, depending on the storefront/wholesale distributor, e.g., sales recorded from March 1 to March 31 will be paid to the publisher between April 30 to early July.

Author Payments

Payment to the author is calculated from the amount received by the publisher. In other words, they can't pay you until they get paid. Terms of author payments vary by publisher and will be stipulated in your publishing contract (e.g., quarterly, semi-annually, annually) and royalty rate (percentage). There is no "standard" term or percentage, though e-books typically earn a higher royalty rate than print. If you are self-published, you are considered the publisher.

Literary agents are paid the contract-designated percentage, e.g., 15% of your royalties, including any advances. This amount is deducted from your share of royalties, *not* the retailer, wholesale distributor, or publisher's share.

Advances

Most writers assume that contracts include an advance against future royalties, paid on signing (or a percentage on signing and the balance on publication) but, at least according to the *Sisters in Crime Business of Books Survey* (2022) (#AR), that's not always the case. In fact, 50% of published authors and 90% of pre-published (debut) authors did not receive an advance.

Of course, that's just one survey, but it's still worthy of mention. If you are paid an advance, and don't earn it out, you won't have to repay the amount, but you also won't receive any further income from that book, regardless of timeline.

Let's take an advance of $1,500 as an example. At the end of five years (or any length of time), your book earned just $800 in royalties. You won't have to pay back the $650 difference (the publisher accepts that as a loss), but you will also not be paid any additional money. Be grateful. You were paid $650 for sales you didn't make.

AND BEFORE WE GET TO THE NITTY GRITTY...

Unlike a "regular" job where no one would dream to ask you how much you earn, you *will* be asked, because no one thinks it is an inappropriate question. I'm not talking about sharing with other authors over drinks at a conference or reporting your annual sales as a means of combating pay inequity. I'm talking about nosey neighbors, your best friend's husband's cousin, even strangers you meet at a backyard barbecue. Be prepared to be asked the question, often when you least expect it. How, or if, you choose to answer it, is your call.

CALCULATING ROYALTIES

Traditional and/or hybrid publishers calculate royalties in one of three ways: Net Receipts, Gross Receipts, or Cover Price. Details on (royalties based on) Cover Price are included under "When It's Not POD" a bit later in this chapter. For now, here's a breakdown on Net and Gross Receipts:

NET RECEIPTS (ALSO CALLED NET SALES): Net Receipts are defined as the total dollar amount received by the Publisher (aka Publisher Compensation) from the wholesale or retail sales of the work during that royalty period, minus any fees (such as PayPal, wire transfer, and other bank fees associated with the sales). In the first example I've assumed that the author is unagented.

EXAMPLE
Publisher Compensation $50.00
Less Bank Fee ($10.00)
Net Receipt $40.00
$40.00 (Net Receipt) x 30% (Royalty Rate) = $12.00
Author Earns: $12.00

GROSS RECEIPTS: The total dollar amount that is received by the publisher (Publisher Compensation) *without* deductions. In the next example, I've assumed the author has an agent.

EXAMPLE
Publisher Compensation $50.00
Gross Receipt $50.00
$50.00 (Gross Receipt) x 30% (Royalty Rate) = $15.00
Less 15% Agent Commission ($ 2.25)
Author Earns: $12.75

PUBLISHER COMPENSATION

You, as the author, will either be paid based on your publisher's net receipts (also known as net sales) or gross receipts. Unless you are self-published (and therefore acting not only as the author, but also the publisher), you will only earn a percentage of the Publisher's Compensation. That percentage will be clearly defined in your contract.

At this point you might be wondering how Publisher Compensation is calculated, and the answer is, "it depends."

DIGITAL/E-BOOK ROYALTIES

The online bookseller is the first in line to take a piece of your royalty pie. Online booksellers include Apple Books, Kindle

(Amazon), Kobo (Rakuten Kobo), NOOK (Barnes & Noble), and others.

E-book royalties are based on the sale price of the book, e.g., a book regularly priced at $9.99 but discounted to $2.99 for a promotion will earn a royalty based on the $2.99 sale price.

Additionally, e-book royalties typically have tiered pricing, once again based on the sale price of a book. Here are two examples:

E-BOOK PRICED LESS THAN $2.99 OR MORE THAN $9.99

- Online seller deducts 65% of the sale price of the book
- Publisher compensation = 35% of the sale price of the book

EXAMPLE A (<$2.99)
Sale Price $1.99
Bookseller deducts 65% = $1.29
Publisher compensation @ 35% = $ 0.70

EXAMPLE B (>$2.99)
Sale Price $12.99
Bookseller deducts 65% = $8.44
Publisher compensation @ 35% = $4.55

E-BOOK PRICED BETWEEN $2.99 AND $9.99

- Online seller deducts 30% of sale price
- Publisher compensation = 70% of sale price

EXAMPLE

Sale Price $7.99

Bookseller deducts 30% = $2.40

Publisher compensation @ 70% = 5.59

Note that where an aggregator (a multi-distribution sales channel, such as Draft2Digital) is used, the aggregator will reduce Publisher Compensation by approximately 10%. Aggregators are often used for less common markets, as well as subscription-based digital services, and for e-book distribution to libraries and institutions.

PRINT-ON-DEMAND ROYALTIES

Independent publishers operate on a print-on-demand (POD) basis; they simply can't afford to sponsor huge print runs in the hope your book will sell in massive quantities. The same holds true for hybrid publishers. And, of course, if you choose to self-publish, POD is the only option in your arsenal. When determining POD royalties, you'll need to factor in two additional steps:

PRINT CHARGE: The actual cost to print the book, calculated by page count (cost per page) and type of ink (standard black and white or upgrade to color). Trim size (e.g., 6" x 9"), cover finish (matte or glossy), and choice of interior paper color (white or cream) do not impact the cost. The quality of the paper (regular, recycled, or premium) will.

WHOLESALE DISCOUNT: The percentage of trade discount off the suggested retail price, offered to booksellers to purchase your book for the resale market. For print-on-demand (POD), the recommended trade discount is 55% (40% to the retailer and 15% to the POD publisher.) Any amount below 55% is known in the industry as a "short discount," and reduces incentive to stock your book. However, unless you have a reasonable expectation for a large volume of brick-and-mortar orders, it can be worth going "short." That's because even if a bookstore won't stock your book on their shelves (and let's face it, unless you are a known commodity, they aren't about to, no matter how great the discount or what else you might be told), they will almost always order a non-returnable copy in at a customer's request. You'll still need to offer a reasonable wholesale discount, e.g., 40% (meaning 25% to the retailer and 15% to POD publisher).

POD EXAMPLE

This example assumes a retail list price of $21.99, a page count of 400, and a print charge of $6.88 per book.

Retail list price $21.99
Less wholesale discount @55% = ($12.09)
Wholesale price = $9.90 (retail less discount)
Minus print charge = ($6.88)
Publisher compensation: $3.02 (wholesale less print charge)

Your jaw may have dropped by this point. Surely for a book that sells for $21.99 the publisher must earn more than $3.02? Because that would mean an author with a POD publisher would earn only a percentage of that amount. Sadly, it's true. In most cases, the print royalty percentage paid by a publisher will be 40% or less, meaning author earnings on a book retailing for $21.99 will be, at best, $1.21.

Eye-opening, isn't it? It also explains why the cost of paperbacks has escalated so rapidly in the past few years. A 400-page trade paperback retailing at $29.99 will have the same print cost of $6.88 as one retailing for $21.99.

But take heart. Even if all an author earns is *one single dollar per sale*, a book that becomes a million-copy bestseller will make that author a millionaire. Sure, the odds are long, and maybe they even seem insurmountable, but you didn't come this far to give up on the dream, did you? Believe in the dream, and maybe, just maybe, it will believe in you.

WHEN IT'S NOT POD

POD has become the gold standard for most independent publishers, regardless of size, but that's not the case with traditional publishing houses, aka the Big Five, which produce print runs versus print on demand. That said, they expect to lose money on one out of every five books they publish (meaning they've printed more copies than they will sell at a profit). Because of that, you might assume the percentage of royalties paid per sale are significantly less than their independent counterparts.

But are they?

These contracts typically pay an author anywhere from 4% to 8% of the print cover price. Simple math tells us that 4% of a book selling for $21.99 will net the author $0.87 per book. At 8%, the author will earn $1.76 per copy—roughly the same as your POD publisher. The difference? Your odds of selling a million copies are far more likely if you've landed a "Big Five" contract and the marketing machine behind it. Your odds of landing a Big Five contract...well, that's another story.

WHAT ABOUT RETURNS?

You've probably returned a book or two in your time without giving it much thought. Now that you are thinking of it, though, it makes sense that if you return a book, the publisher would be charged back the original amount of compensation. That's true for e-books, but when it comes to print, things can get more expensive.

Let's take our previous print example, where the publisher compensation was $3.72. In that case, the publisher would be charged back the wholesale price of $9.90. However, if the publisher allowed physical returns (vs. an option of Return/Destroy) there will be an additional shipping and handling charge, and the quality of any returned books will not be guaranteed. Because book returns can be costly, the decision to opt in should be carefully considered. However, unless you are self-published, it's unlikely the decision will be left to you. This is especially true of large presses, where returns are an inevitable part of life, though it may also hold true for independent publishers.

Whatever your situation, the terms regarding returns will be clearly outlined in your publishing contract, e.g., "Net copies sold shall mean the number of copies sold, less any returned (including copies destroyed or otherwise deemed destroyed) or those sold at or below publishing cost." The latter refers to those clearance bin copies you'll find at bookstores, where the price has been marked down to a fraction of the original list.

You might be offered "book return insurance" by a hybrid or small, independent press. Since there are no insurance companies that offer this type of coverage, the "insurance" is provided by the publisher in exchange for a set amount (upfront and usually quite steep) paid by the author. Exercise extreme caution before purchasing, and before you do, ask yourself: Do you anticipate multiple bookstores nationwide to stock your book in large quantities? If you're a known commodity and the answer is yes, then go for it. If your expectations are more modest, save your money. Make your book non-returnable (despite any pressure tactics to the contrary) and move on. There will be better ways to spend your hard-earned cash.

ADVERTISING & PROMOTION

TALKING about advertising and promotion might seem a bit like putting the cart before the horse, especially if you're planning on following a traditional publishing path, but the one thing many authors struggle with most is marketing.

True, if you land a contract with a large press, odds are a publicity team will put together a solid package for you. That said, the A-listers will get the bulk of time, money, and attention, and you'll still be required to do more than your fair share of the heavy lifting (and paying). That "fair share" increases exponentially as the size of the press decreases. Hybrid publishers can and do offer marketing support, however that will get costly. The more you can take control of on your own, the better. Should you decide to go indie, it will all fall on you.

AUTHOR PHOTO

You'll use this for many things: your website, inside your book, guest blogs, newspaper articles, conference catalogs…the list goes on. A professional headshot is a worthwhile investment, and while you want to put your best face forward, ask them to go easy on the filters and photoshopping. The idea is to be recognized from your author photo.

BLOGS

Whatever publishing path you choose, a personal blog can be the first step in building a following. Even better, outside of the time invested to write the posts, it's free. While it's never too late, having an active blog before you begin the querying process can count as a point in your favor. "Here," an agent or publisher might think, "is an author invested in their future."

Even if you don't have a blog, following one or more writing/genre-related blogs can allow you to gradually cultivate a relationship with those bloggers by sharing their posts on social media and/or leaving insightful comments on posts that resonate with you. When the time comes to celebrate your own book news, you can legitimately approach that blogger for a spot or tag them in a social post, which they will (hopefully) share. Start by following as many writing-related or genre-specific blogs as you can comfortably handle without turning this exercise into a part-time job, understanding that the expectation is never that you interact with, or share, every single post. This is following, not stalking.

In addition to individual blogs, there are also blog tours and blitzes. Blog tours are an online version of a traditional book tour, designed to promote books that have already been, or are about to be, published. Much more popular since the COVID-19 pandemic, these typically run for a period of five to ten days, with each post offering original content. Blitzes, on the other hand, feature several blogs posting the same content at the same time. Both can be arranged by a blog tour company, of which there are many, which will find willing hosts. Here's the sticky wicket: you, as the author, will be required to create the content, which takes time and effort. There are no free lunches on the promo circuit.

Because blog tour companies list links to their current and upcoming tours and blitzes, you'll have an opportunity to vet them using your own specific criteria, e.g., were the blog hosts a good fit for the novel being promoted, or were they just trying to fill up available slots, regardless of the genre or sub-genre?

The bottom line? You may not use a blog tour service for many months yet, if at all, but at the very least you'll gain a better understanding of the blog and blitz tour business. As a rule, tours trend towards gaining visibility vs. selling books, and it's unlikely that you'll break even on your investment, however modest.

ONLINE / SOCIAL PRESENCE

Never underestimate the power of social media, or the effort you'll have to put in to keep up with the changing times (there's always something newer and shinier…remember MySpace?) and understand your target demographic. Facebook remains a favorite with an older crowd, and, at the moment, TikTok tends to attract a younger demographic. Nevertheless, social platforms like Instagram, TikTok, Twitter, Facebook, and others can be a great way to connect with readers. In fact, BookTok (a term coined for the book-related content on TikTok) has been credited with bumping print sales in 2022, and Instagram's bookstagrammers have become an integral part of the bookish community.

While regular social media posts are free, there are always options to pay for advertising or boosting a post beyond your existing followers. Targeting criteria makes it easy to get your content in front of individuals with specific interests that line up with your book to find new readers. Targeting can also be defined by a specific geographic area, which can be helpful when promoting in-person events. Before you head down this path, you'll need to understand audience targeting, the difference between clicks, impressions, and clickthrough rates, and the cost of each. Here's a quick primer:

- Clicks: The number of people who click on your ad.
- Impressions: The number of people who saw your ad.
- Clickthrough Rate (CTR): Clicks divided by impressions.
- Example: CTR = 50 (Clicks) ÷ 1,000 (Impressions) = 0.05 x 100 (percentage) = 5% CTR

While there is no hard and fast rule, a CTR of 4 to 5% is generally considered good, and 3% or less means something is lacking. In the above scenario of 1,000 impressions at 5%, it also means that 950 people who saw your ad did not click on it.

A few pennies per click can also add up quickly, and it's important to remember that not all clicks equal sales. How often have you inadvertently clicked on an ad? Or clicked on it and then thought, "no, I don't think so." And you really don't want to pay per impression.

While some authors have success (meaning they'll recoup their investment and make a few dollars), advertising on social media can be a bit like going to a casino. At the end of the day, the house usually wins.

There are ways, however, to increase your odds. Creativity (whether that's a static post or a clever video), not salesmanship, is also essential. Repeated "enough about my book, here's more about my book" campaigns will turn off readers. In my experience, balancing personal posts and/or writing quotes/wisdoms with promotion is the most effective strategy to build a strong and engaged social following that benefits you. Don't forget, it doesn't have to go viral to be effective. A post that resonates with people, whether a book review, something about your writing journey, or a piece of writing advice, that gets shared by enough people can work wonders in attracting potential new readers to your account and building your dedicated following.

I'd also suggest collaborating with other authors to promote each other's work. One way to do this is to join or create what's known as a "street team" (a dedicated group of readers who like your work and are interested in helping promote your books) (#AR). I'm often more inclined to purchase a book recommended to me by a friend or author whose books I enjoy, than when the author is pitching their own book. My guess is, you're much the same.

Third Party Marketing

Yet another option is to hire a book publicist or a promotion or marketing firm, someone who will take care of the vetting and promoting for you (and may even write some, or all, of the content for an added fee). Because this involves the most hands-on involvement by a third party, it should also be the most personalized. As such, it will be your most expensive option, often in the thousands of dollars.

As with any marketing plan, prices vary widely and results are mixed. Obtain references and examples of past promotions and ensure that expectations on both sides are clearly defined in writing. A publicist is usually focused on traditional media, whereas a marketing firm will consider multiple promotional avenues.

YouTube

There are several advertising alternatives to blogging, including paid advertising, newsletters, and promotional materials, such as pens, postcards, and bookmarks. And if you're in a better position to invest time than money, YouTube is another great option that can provide some variety to your creative outlets and be an effective way to put a face to your author brand. Here you can explore the same variety of content as on a blog—book trailers, writing tips, and day-in-the-life videos are just a few examples of how viewers can get to know you and your book, and they're easy to share on social media.

BOOK LAUNCHES

It's fun to dream, right? Even pre-publication, put some thought into the kind of book launch event you'd like to have. More and more, these are happening virtually, which has its benefits. Namely, no cost to rent a location or feed your guests in attendance, as well as broadening your potential audience from local to global. But there is no shortage of benefits for in-person launches either—book signings, on-the-spot purchases, face-to-face interaction with readers, and the potential for local media coverage (the best kind of free advertising). If you're unsure of the right fit for you and your book, the best way to learn what you do—and don't—like is to attend some book launches and see for yourself. As an added bonus, you'll be supporting a fellow author, and it's never too early to start networking.

GOODREADS

Many readers, including me, use Goodreads to rate and review books. Setting up an author profile is free, as is adding your book's information to the website. If you have a blog, you can link that directly to your Goodreads author profile page. There's also an area on your profile for questions from readers you can answer (or make up a couple of your own), as well as multiple reader groups you can join (typically defined by genre of interest, e.g., cozy mystery), as well as other promotional opportunities. If you aren not reviewing books on there already, now's the time to start. It's a free and easy way to be a good and active member of the literary community, and besides, you shouldn't expect reviews if you're unwilling to give them yourself (#AR).

AUTHOR CENTRAL

You've read author bios and editorial reviews of books on Amazon, but did you know those were created using Amazon's Author Central? In addition to providing book stats, the platform allows you to post your bio, photos, and share your blog feed (#AR).

BOOKBUB

Start by joining as a reader, reviewing, and recommending books. Once your book is published, creating an author profile is free. BookBub also offers a Partners blog with advice on marketing, as well as paid advertising options (#AR).

MEDIA

There are many choices at your disposal when it comes to media, which range from bank-breaking to completely free.

When I worked as a magazine editor, I appreciated a professionally written press release, but that didn't mean the magazine used every one that landed in my mailbox, whether it came from a PR professional or an individual. In fact, regardless of the magazine, press releases were considered "filler," a way to fill in a blank spot that had been left open in the hope a last-minute ad might be booked. As such, relatively few were used (unless, of course, our sales team could talk the PR pro or individual into a paid ad). Before you choose the paid PR route, ask for PDFs of recent examples, including which newspapers and/or magazine the press release appeared in.

My personal experience is that local media will usually include a press release of mine if I direct it to the correct individual and personalize the request as a local author. But hey, I'm a writer, so I write my own. Then again, so are you.

You can also look at paid advertising with newspapers and magazines. If you aren't a graphic designer yourself, most outlets offer creative work at an hourly fee in addition to the cost of the ad space. And with so many newspapers moving to digital platforms, there are plenty of options for reasonably priced digital ads on their websites and newsletters that are more affordable than print ads. These can also be hyperlinked directly to your online store or website. Digital ads also often have a longer shelf life than print ads in say, a weekly or daily paper, giving you more bang for your buck.

While press releases have no guarantee of getting published, advertorials do. Often overlooked but a common tactic in marketing, these are paid articles that appear in a newspaper as regular content but give you more control over the messaging of the story. Ever notice the words "sponsored content" at the top of a news article? It's this cleverly disguised form of advertising. The cost varies by publication, and by length, but you may decide this tactic is money well spent.

Other potential options include regional television or radio; a cable TV provider might have a channel in search of local news, a local radio station might offer programming to showcase authors.

Podcasts are also popular, and they are growing in leaps and bounds. Many smaller start-ups are looking for content. Some writing associations and libraries have a dedicated YouTube channel that includes interviews with members or local authors. You might even consider trying to do your own.

You are not there—yet—but it never hurts to research your

best resources going forward. If nothing else, you can spend a few hours daydreaming, and there's nothing wrong with that.

One final caveat: always do your due diligence *and then some* before hiring any outside firm or individual. Starting the process pre-publication can protect you from being rushed or pressured into making an uninformed decision.

Promises are cheap. Advertising isn't.

THE WRITE LIFE

ASSOCIATIONS

It sometimes seems as if there are as many writing and author-related associations as there are writers, and deciding which ones to join can be overwhelming. National or regional? Big or small? Most organizations charge a membership fee, but the fees can be considered a tax-deductible business expense.

The first thing to remember is that while some associations offer lifetime memberships, joining one doesn't have to be a lifelong commitment. Associations most valuable to you as an emerging author may hold less value to you post publication. The reverse is also true. Start with a trial membership, if offered, and an annual membership if one is not. A partial list of writing associations can be found in Additional Resources: Resources by Section.

From international, North American, and national to regional and local levels, the breadth and depth of associations varies widely, as do the types of membership benefits. Your local arts council might have a critique group that meets on a regular basis. A larger organization might offer grants for professional development, educational programs, and webinars and presentations. Beyond the craft, larger organizations like the Authors Guild offers helpful resources to help writers at any point in their career understand the more complex, but no less important, aspects of the business, such as copyright and contracts.

Here's a sample of members-only benefits you might find:

- Access to liability and/or health insurance.
- Author bio page on association's website.
- Blog page.
- Contract advice.
- Critique groups.
- Directory of additional resources.
- Discounts on professional services (editing, design, printing, etc.).
- Discounts on writing-related magazine subscriptions.
- Educational courses.
- Genre-related reports.
- Grants for professional development.
- In-person and/or virtual meetings.
- Lending library for writing-related reference books.
- Marketing memos.
- Member magazines and/or newsletters
- Membership badge (for website use).
- Members' directory.
- Members only website access for exclusive content.
- Mentorship programs.
- Online discussion forum (such as discussion boards and online digests, such as Groups.io).
- Online and/or brick-and-mortar store for book sales.
- Reciprocal membership discounts.
- Regional/local chapters.
- Reports and/or surveys on publishing.
- Social media promotion.

- Sponsorship of events, conferences, and conventions.
- Virtual meetings.
- Webinars.
- Weekly write-ins.
- Workshops.
- Writing awards (for published novels and/or unpublished manuscripts).
- Writing contests.
- Writing tips and advice.

A less tangible benefit, but equally important consideration, is that memberships can serve as proof to agents and/or publishers that you are serious about your craft. Be sure to include any affiliations in your bio and query letter.

Many associations also actively seek volunteers to work on committees and special projects. Some even offer select positions on their Board of Directors for unpublished authors, so don't be afraid to ask if you're interested in getting involved. Volunteering can be an invaluable experience when it comes to networking and understanding the behind-the-scenes world of book publishing.

Points to Ponder

Top Five: Write down a list of the five must-have elements you want from a writing association membership. Think of this exercise in the same way you might approach buying a house (must have three bedrooms and two bathrooms). These are your non-negotiables.

Mushy Middle: This is your wish list (I'd really like granite countertops and stainless-steel appliances, but I could live with laminate and a white fridge and stove.)

BOTTOM FIVE: Finally, list your "Never gonna use it/don't care" list (e.g., soundproofed, musician-friendly garage).

Once you've made your lists, consider the following:

MEMBERSHIP TYPE: Look at the membership categories the association offers, specifically those offered to unpublished authors. Do benefits pander more to the published, with a trinket or two to the aspiring, or is it an equal split? Are there other opportunities (such as volunteerism)? How easy will it be to commute your membership to "Published Author" status?

COST OF ADMISSION: Are there trial memberships? Do they have a refund policy? Are pro-rated annual memberships available if you join mid-year? Is there a way to test drive your membership?

TERRITORY: National, regional, or local? Is the association genre-specific (e.g., mystery), geared to independently published and/or self-published authors, or is the focus broader, all-encompassing? What's more important at this stage of your career? Can one membership satisfy all (or at least most) of your wants? Or are you ready to mix and match by joining two or more associations?

VOLUNTEERISM: Local arts groups often require a minimum number of volunteer hours as part of the membership requirement. Are you ready for that commitment? On the other hand, larger associations may not offer volunteer spots to unpublished authors (though many do).

There are no right or wrong associations, and no right or wrong answers. There are only the answers that work best for you at this point in your writing journey.

After all, this is *your* path to publication.

"FREE" MONEY

Contests, awards, and grants. The very thought of them conjures up images of "free" money and skyrocketing to professional success. But submitting to contests and awards usually requires an entry fee, and grants often require an extensive application process. Here's a quick look at what to expect:

Writing Contests & Awards

A good place to start your search is the *Poets & Writers* website. Not only does it showcase a fairly comprehensive list of the contests out there, *Poets & Writers* (#AR) reviews the practices and policies of each contest before including it, which is helpful (sadly, not all writing contests are legit). Many writing associations, especially those that are genre-specific, also sponsor awards, usually without a membership requirement. But are they worth entering?

They can be. Winning, being short- or long-listed, even getting an honorable mention, can make a nice addition to your bio. Additionally, some competitions will offer a brief critique to non-winning entries of unpublished manuscripts or short stories. If they do, put a checkmark in the plus column. Honest professional feedback is invaluable as you continue to hone your craft.

POINTS TO PONDER

YOUR WHY: Are you looking for validation? Feedback? Prize money? Bragging rights? Honest evaluation? Or just someplace to send your stuff to say you tried?

APPLICATION PROCESS: Rigorous and time-consuming? Or simple and straightforward?

ENTRY FEE: If not free, does the reward, financial or otherwise, justify the cost?

JUDGING PROCESS: Judges' names are often anonymous, but the process should be clearly defined and transparent.

PAST WINNERS: Legitimate competitions list the names of past winners, and often the names of those who were shortlisted.

WHO: Who is sponsoring the contest? How long have they been doing it? What's *their* reason for supporting it?

FINE PRINT: The part where you usually just scroll down and click "I agree" without reading it? Read it. Then treat it like a contract—because it is. What publication rights are you signing away by entering? What about if you win or are shortlisted? The devil really is in the details.

GRANTS

Writing-related grants typically come in two forms: project-based or professional development. Whether backed by local, regional, or federal government initiatives or non-profit foundations, eligibility is often measured by your publication track record, meaning unpublished authors need not apply. That said, there are always exceptions. An excellent primer on grants and grant writing (which is a skill in itself) can be found on Jane Friedman's website (#AR).

POINTS TO PONDER

REQUIREMENTS: Do you have the qualifications required for eligibility?

CHANCE OF SUCCESS: What percentage or number of applicants receive grants? Are certain ethnic or diverse groups or geographical areas (e.g., those in rural or remote regions) given priority?

APPLICATION PROCESS: In doing a time/cost benefit analysis, does the amount of a (possible) grant warrant the time spent to complete the paperwork?

MENTORSHIP PROGRAMS

Mentorship programs are popping up more and more online. These can be a great way to build your network with fellow writers as well as connect with industry professionals who can lend some insights into how you might follow in their footsteps. These are often free to enter and have different opportunities for specific genres or underrepresented authors. Finished manuscripts can be submitted for consideration, much like pitching literary agents, and participating mentors will select projects they feel they can help to improve with one-on-one coaching.

POINTS TO PONDER

ASSOCIATIONS: Many writing associations offer mentorship programs. If this is important to you, look for that as a member benefit when researching which one(s) to potentially join.

SCAMMER ALERT: Be mindful to watch for scams whenever fees are requested. I can't say it enough, always do your due diligence.

WRITING CONFERENCES & CONVENTIONS

As an aspiring author, you've probably been given advice to attend a writing conference or convention. Well-meant, but not that helpful, given the sheer number to choose from. As with associations, your wants and needs will evolve over time. So, too, will your expectations from a writing conference or convention. If you're unpublished, you may be looking for an opportunity to pitch your book to an agent, whereas once published, you'll be looking for ways to promote your book to readers.

While the terms are often used interchangeably, there are differences between the core objective of conferences and conventions. Let's begin by defining those differences:

CONFERENCES

The primary purpose of an industry-specific and, in the case of writing, usually genre-specific, conference is the exchange of information with an educational component, a venue where attendees can learn and better themselves professionally. For example, in addition to networking opportunities, a conference might offer master classes, craft-related seminars or workshops, breakout sessions, presentations, manuscript critiques, author-led panel or roundtable discussions, and live agent and/or publisher pitch sessions.

Most conferences also host a debut author program or an awards banquet and dinner. Both offer excellent opportunities, even if you're not a debut author or eligible for award consideration. A debut author may be very willing to share their publishing journey with you. As for the awards nominees and winners, reading award-nominated books and meeting those who penned them can be an education in itself. In my experience, authors in all stages of their careers are more than willing to take a few minutes to chat.

Registration for conferences is open to readers, authors, and aspiring authors, with a bestselling guest (or guests) of honor on the program to draw attendees. They typically take place over three to four days. Some offer one-day passes or fee-per-session options. Conferences are usually held in the same city each year.

CONVENTIONS

Most writing conventions are billed as fan-based, meaning the primary objective is to introduce readers to authors and vice versa. In addition to author interviews, there are author-led panel discussions, however the emphasis generally falls on showcasing attending authors vs. educating attendees. Some conventions will include an educational component, such as a workshop, seminar, or master class, but these are typically held prior to the start of the convention so as not to interfere with scheduled programming.

Similar to conferences, most conventions also host a debut author program and awards banquet and dinner, and the same networking parameters found in conventions also apply.

As with conferences, convention registration is open to

readers, authors, and aspiring authors, with bestselling guests of honor on the program to draw attendees. They typically take place over three to four days, and some may offer one-day passes. A key difference is that conventions are often held in a different city each year, with discounted or group sightseeing excursions offered to attendees. At the end of the day, conventions are more about entertainment than education.

POINTS TO PONDER

LOCATION: Do you want something close to home? Or would you prefer to combine business with pleasure and visit a place on your travel wish list, perhaps combining it with a family or solo vacation? Your accountant can explain the ins and outs of what you can write off, but registration fees, travel, hotel accommodations for the length of the conference or convention, and a portion of meals are, in general, tax-deductible expenses. Sightseeing excursions and additional nights or expenses are not.

TOTAL COST: Think registration fee, travel, travel insurance, hotel, meals. Registration fees are usually tiered, with early-bird pricing that escalates as you get closer to the event. The earlier you book the less you'll pay, but you'll want to check the cancellation policy. Terms and conditions vary widely. Some conferences offer scholarships based on financial need, though there will be an application process, and it's not guaranteed.

NETWORKING: Both conferences and conventions offer networking opportunities, though a smaller venue is generally more conducive to making one-on-one personal connections.

YOUR #1 WHY: Pitching to an agent or publisher? Honing your craft? Mix and mingling with other authors, both published and aspiring? Defining your *why* is essential to the planning process to get the most out of your experience.

TYPE OF EVENT: Are you interested in writing in general, or would you prefer an event that has a genre-specific focus (e.g., romance, mystery, sci-fi)? In my experience, there are far more that are focused. Additionally, genre-specific events will introduce you to like-minded individuals, providing an opportunity to network with readers and other authors, aspiring and published.

WARDROBE: You can't go wrong with business casual (this is a business meeting, after all), with layers to accommodate unpredictable conference room temperatures which can range from frigidly air conditioned to hot and stuffy. Bring something a bit dressier for the banquet evenings. Not wedding fancy, but a step up from your daytime duds. I'd also recommend comfortable shoes.

VIRTUAL OR LIVE: Many conventions now offer virtual options. The good news is the cost will be minimal (no travel-associated costs). The bad news is networking opportunities are minimal or non-existent. That said, virtual offerings are a way to dip your toe in the water to get a feel for the experience without diving into the deep end.

Pro Tip: Conference and convention organizers will book a block of rooms at the host hotel to offer discounted pricing, but the number of available rooms will be limited and booking at the time of registration is usually recommended. Since most networking takes place after the day's scheduled programming ends, staying at the host hotel (if financially feasible) may enhance your overall experience. At the very least it will allow you a place to take a quiet (and often much-needed) break between sessions. Don't discount this as a value-add: conferences and conventions can be exhilarating, but being "on" 24/7 for three or four days is also exhausting.

FINDING YOUR FIT

By now you've made your list of wishes, wants, and whys, and are ready for the conference/ convention when and where. But where do you start?

If you're on social media or part of an online writing group, that's a good place to pose the question. Associations, too, will often endorse, sponsor, or supply a list of conferences and conventions. A simple Google search with keywords like "mystery conference" and the year is sure to bring up a laundry list of suggestions. Too many? Filter your search by adding defined geographic areas.

Attending conferences or conventions isn't for everyone, especially in view of the time and cost considerations, not to mention that the truly introverted writer might find it all too intimidating. But remember this: once you've been published (and that's the dream, right?) you may be required (or plan) to attend one in the future, and be invited to be part of a panel discussion. Watching and learning from the sidelines is a painless way to start planning for your turn.

Let the journey begin.

ADDITIONAL RESOURCES

TALKING THE TALK

Advance: The payment paid by a publisher on signing and/or publication in advance of any future royalties (monies) earned.

Advertorial: Paid newspaper article that appears as regular content, often used in marketing strategies. Rates vary per publication, and the purchaser has final say on what is published.

Aggregator: A one-stop online distributor that will list your book with several online booksellers, as well as library and subscription services.

Alpha readers: Readers who provide detailed and constructive feedback on your unpolished first draft about premise, plot, characters, and other technical elements.

ARCs: Advanced reader copies.

Author bio: A brief description about the author written in third person, including information relevant to your story or work as an author, often found at the back of a book.

Beta readers (betas): Readers familiar with your genre/sub-genre who critique finished manuscripts before they are published.

Blog: A website or webpage that is updated regularly with content from one or more writers on a specific topic or theme.

Blurb: Praise for a book included inside or on the cover.

Book Industry Standards and Communications (BISAC): These are codes that indicate the categories and subcategories of your book to retailers, distributors, and librarians so they know where it should be shelved. BISAC codes are generated by categories chosen by the publisher prior to retail upload.

Book launch: Virtual or in-person event or series of events to promote the release of your book.

Brick-and-mortar: Refers to the physical location of a business where products are sold.

Clicks: The number of people who click on your ad.

Clickthrough (CTR): The number of people who click on your ad, divided by the number of impressions (people who saw it).

Climax: The final battle in a manuscript that determines who (or what) wins established conflicts.

Comparable titles: Also called "comps," these are books that are similar to yours in tone, theme, setting, vibe, etc., ideally published within the last five years, and with a proven track record. Comp titles are typically included in query letters and pitches to agents and publishers.

Conference: Virtual or in-person event with an educational component for attendees to learn and better themselves professionally. Often include networking opportunities, master classes, smaller seminars or workshops, manuscript critiques, author-led panels, live agent/publisher pitch sessions, and more.

Contract: Legal agreement detailing the exchange of products and services.

Convention: Fan-based in-person or virtual event usually taking place over several days to introduce readers to authors and vice versa, with the emphasis on showcasing authors. Activities usually include author interviews, author-led panel discussions, and networking.

Copyright: The exclusive legal ownership of artistic material. Laws vary from one country to the next. Permission is required by the copyright owner to copy or use these works.

Closed for submissions: Period in which an agent or publisher is not accepting new pitches. You should not pitch to an agent or publisher during this time.

Critique group: Writers who connect on a regular basis to share their work for the purpose of remaining accountable to their project, exchanging feedback, and improving their craft.

Critique partner: Writer you connect with on a regular basis one-on-one to exchange feedback on each other's work, encouragement, and remain accountable to your respective projects.

Denouement: Following the climax, this is the final part of the narrative arc where the different threads of the story come together, and conflicts are resolved.

Direct to consumer: Sales method from author to customer with no middleman, e.g., at a book fair.

Domain name: A website address (e.g.: judypenzsheluk.com). For authors, it is ideally your name, plus an extension like .com, but if you have a common first and last name, you'll have to get more creative.

Earn out: When book sales equal or exceed the advance paid to the author.

E-commerce site: A website that has the function for people to buy and sell physical and digital products and services, like paperback books, e-books, and related merchandise.

Elevator pitch: A way to effectively share your expertise, credentials, and project quickly with agents and/or publishers.

Falling action: The period between denouement and climax.

Full: A request from an agent or publisher for the complete manuscript.

Galley proof: A preliminary, formatted digital version of your soon-to-be-published novel.

Genre: Category of story, e.g., mystery, romance, science fiction.

Hybrid author: An author who is both traditionally and self-published.

Hybrid publisher: A reputable publisher that offers assisted self-publishing, sometimes referred to as "pay-to-play," with editorial standards and gatekeeping. Not to be confused with vanity publishing, though some vanity presses will identify themselves as hybrid publishers.

Impressions: The number of people who see your ad.

Inciting incident: The event that sets the action in motion, often leading your protagonist on a new course.

Independently published author: Writer who has self-published their book(s).

Independent publisher: Independently owned and managed, not part of any larger publishing house and in no way associated with any of their smaller imprints.

ISBN: International Standard Book Number is a unique code assigned to each commercial book that contains the publication details of each edition and format.

Jacket copy: Also known as the retail blurb or back of book blurb, this is a teaser meant to hook readers.

KDP – Kindle Direct Publishing: Amazon's publishing platform.

Landing page: A standalone web page potential readers will be redirected to from linked ads, emails, or other digital locations.

Loglines: Concise, engaging summary of the essence of your plot in one to two sentences.

Manuscript evaluation: An unbiased review of your novel's strengths and weaknesses.

Microblogging: Similar in content to a blog, with a photo and brief message on a specific topic or theme, often shared via social media.

Micro publisher: Typically a one- or two-person operation, often started as a way of self-publishing the owner's work(s).

Narrative arc: The chronological structure of one single story or a connected series that includes the exposition or starting action, inciting incident, rising action, climax, falling action, resolution, and denouement.

Orphaned: A term used when an author's publishing contract is terminated, also known as reversion of rights.

Orphaned work: A term that refers to a book where copyright exists, but where the copyright owner is either unknown or cannot be located.

Partial: A request from an agent or publisher for a partial manuscript, e.g., first 50,000 words.

Pay-to-play: Another term for "hybrid publisher," which offers assisted self-publishing.

Pitch: A concise presentation of your idea to generate agent and/or publisher interest.

Pitch contest: Often on social media platforms like Twitter, authors are invited to pitch their story to participating agents or publishers for consideration of representation or publication.

Pitch sessions: Done virtually or in person, these are opportunities for unagented authors to pitch their book in a controlled setting with more direct access to agents and/or publishers than submitting based on their submission guidelines.

Platform: Your vehicle to reach your readers with news about your work. Platform can be comprised of one or more channels, such as a website, social media account(s), and/or blog.

Press release (PR): A pre-packaged statement about your book and all pertinent details, distributed to relevant newspapers and magazines.

Print-on-demand (POD): A publishing platform where books are printed when ordered, without minimum quantity requirements.

Protected work: Artistic work that falls under copyright laws.

Public domain: All creative work that no longer falls under or is protected by copyright; permission is not required to copy or use these works.

Publisher Compensation: The amount a publisher is paid by the digital storefront or distributor.

Publishing imprint: Smaller branches of a larger publishing company to market to different audiences (e.g., Berkley is an imprint under Penguin Random House) and/or the brand used to publish books.

Query letters: Similar to a cover letter when applying to a job, this is a formal letter sent to agents or publishers with a pitch of one specific project when seeking agent representation or publication.

Reversion of rights: Publishing rights granted under the terms of the publishing contract are reversed and returned to the author.

Rising action: Series of events within the narrative arc of a story that outline the roadblocks and conflicts to be overcome.

Royalties: What an author is paid from book sales.

SASE: Self-addressed stamped envelope.

Scrivener: A paid word-processing and outlining program for authors.

Serialized format: Publishing longer work in smaller segments, often done through social publishing platforms, such as Wattpad, Inkitt, or Kindle Vella.

Simultaneous submissions: When an author or agent submits their book for consideration to multiple agents or publishers at one time, without waiting for acceptance or rejection letters.

Social publishing: An avenue for authors to write, publish, and distribute their work in a public or semi-public forum, directly to readers, either by a personal blog or via an established storytelling website.

Street Team: A dedicated group of readers (fans) who like your work and are interested in helping promote your books.

Style sheet: List prepared by an editor with important style and spelling rules throughout your book to maintain consistency.

Sub-genre: A more specific way of categorizing your story type within each genre, e.g., cozy mystery or historical romance.

Submission: The package sent to an agent or publisher for consideration of representation or publication.

Submission guidelines: Included on an agency or publisher's website, instructions that tell you the type of books they accept and how they want your work sent for consideration.

Synopsis: A summary of your novel's narrative arc, including plot twists and the ending, as well as brief descriptions of the key personality traits that define your major characters. Always written in third person, present tense, regardless of how your book is written.

Traditional (Trade Book) Publishers a.k.a. "The Big Five": Major publishing houses Hachette Book Group, HarperCollins, Macmillan Publishers, Penguin Random House, and Simon & Schuster make up the Big Five. Also called "Trad publishers."

Unagented submissions: Pitching your project directly to a publisher without agent representation.

Vanity press: Also referred to as a vanity publisher or subsidy publisher, a disreputable publishing company with limited (usually no) editorial or creative standards, with the sole intent of exploiting the writer. Not to be confused with reputable hybrid (assisted) publishers who vet submissions, though many vanity presses will adopt the hybrid label.

Website developer: Outside company (or individual) hired to build a website. Costs and services vary widely from one developer to the next.

Wish list: List of desired stories or topics that an agent or publisher is interested in receiving.

Works for hire: Creative work made by an employee or independent contractor under an employment contract commissioning the work.

RESOURCES BY SECTION

***This is a list of resources only; no endorsement is being made for any of the firms or services listed.**

PAVING THE WAY

SELF-PUBLISHING (MANAGING EXPECTATIONS)

2018 Authors Guild survey of U.S. professional writers
https://authorsguild.org/news/six-takeaways-from-the-authors-guild-2018-authors-income-survey/
*Survey to be updated in 2023

Sisters in Crime *Business of Books Survey (2022)*
https://www.sistersincrime.org/page/2021BoBS

GETTING DOWN TO BUSINESS

FIRST FIVE STEPS

Book Industry Standards and Communications (BISAC) codes
https://www.bisg.org/complete-bisac-subject-headings-list

UNDERSTANDING COPYRIGHT

The Berne Convention for the Protection of Literary and Artistic Works
https://www.wipo.int/treaties/en/ip/berne/

SECURING A LITERARY AGENT OR PUBLISHER

Association of American Literary Agents
https://aalitagents.org/canon-of-ethics/

Canadian Literary Agents
https://www.writersunion.ca/literary-agents

QueryTracker.net
https://querytracker.net/

QueryLetter.com
https://www.queryletter.com/post/161-examples-of-successful-query-letters-from-famous-author

Publishers Marketplace
https://www.publishersmarketplace.com

UNDERSTANDING YOUR OPTIONS

TRADITIONAL (TRADE BOOK) PUBLISHERS A.K.A. THE BIG FIVE

Current state of the market
https://www.publishersweekly.com/pw/by-topic/industry-news/publisher-news/article/89038-over-the-past-25-years-the-big-publishers-got-bigger-and-fewer.html

Write for Harlequin
https://www.writeforharlequin.com/

INDEPENDENT PUBLISHING

Scams and scammers
https://writerbeware.blog/scam-archive/?utm_source=mailpoet&utm_medium=email&utm_campaign=the-latest-post-from-the-writer-beware-blog_154

Writer Beware by Victoria Strauss
https://writerbeware.blog/

Article: *Whatever Happened to Catstone Books?*
https://writerbeware.blog/2022/11/11/whatever-happened-to-catstone-books/

Mystery Writers of America: Approved Publisher List
https://mysterywriters.org/how-to-become-a-member-of-mwa/approved-publisher-list/

HYBRID/ASSISTED PUBLISHING

The Independent Book Publishers Association's *Hybrid Publisher Criteria* free download
https://www.ibpa-online.org/page/hybrid-publisher-criteria-download

The Alliance of Independent Authors' (ALLi's) *The Best Self-Publishing Services (And the Worst)*
https://selfpublishingadvice.org/best-self-publishing-services/

Cost-benefit analysis of assisted publishing add-ons
https://online.hbs.edu/blog/post/cost-benefit-analysis

SELF-PUBLISHING

- *FORMATTING & SOFTWARE*

Adobe InDesign
https://www.adobe.com/products/indesign.html

Article: Kindlepreneur
https://kindlepreneur.com/how-to-hire-a-book-formatter/

Article: Kobo Writing Life
https://kobowritinglife.zendesk.com/hc/en-us/articles/360058975512

Article: Selfpublishing.com
https://selfpublishing.com/book-formatting-software/

Atticus
https://www.atticus.io

Draft2Digital
https://draft2digital.com/knowledge-base/

Scrivener
https://www.literatureandlatte.com/scrivener/overview

Vellum
https://store.vellum.pub/

- *SALES STATS*

WordsRated
https://wordsrated.com/self-published-book-sales-statistics/

- *TRADEMARK NAME DATABASES*

U.S.: https://www.uspto.gov/trademarks/search

Canada: https://www.canada.ca/en/services/business/start/
choosing-a-business-name-2.html

- *TAXES*

W-8 BEN form
https://www.irs.gov/forms-pubs/about-form-w-8-ben

- *COPYRIGHT*

U.S. General: https://www.copyright.gov/
U.S. Registration: https://www.copyright.gov/registration/

Canada General: https://www.canada.ca/en/services/business/ip/copyright.html

Canada Registration: https://copyright-application-online.com/apply/

- *ISBNs*

U.S.: https://www.bowker.com/isbn-us

Canada: https://www.bac-lac.gc.ca/eng/services/isbn-canada/Pages/isbn-canada.aspx

- *REVIEW SITES*

Kirkus Reviews: https://www.kirkusreviews.com/

Midwest Book Reviews: https://www.midwestbookreview.com/

- *E-BOOK RETAILERS/DISTRIBUTORS*

Amazon (Kindle Direct Publishing): https://kdp.amazon.com/en_US/

Apple (iTunes Connect): https://itunespartner.apple.com/books/

Barnes & Noble Nook (B&N Press): https://press.barnesandnoble.com

D2D https://www.draft2digital.com/Path

Google Play https://play.google.com/books/publish/u/0/

Kobo (Rakuten Kobo): https://writinglife.kobo.com

Untreed Reads https://www.untreedreads.com/
additionalservices/

Universal Book Link
https://books2read.com/links/ubl/create/

Print on Demand – IngramSpark
https://www.ingramspark.com/

Article: *How to Select Keywords for Your Book*
https://www.babelcube.com/how/select-keywords

Book Industry Standards and Communications (BISAC) codes
https://www.bisg.org/BISAC-Subject-Codes-main

- *SERIALIZED PUBLISHING*

Wattpad: https://www.wattpad.com/

Inkitt: https://www.inkitt.com/

Kindle Vella: https://kdp.amazon.com/en_US/help/topic/
GR2L4AHPMQ44HNQ7

- *SOCIAL PUBLISHING*

Article: *How To Choose the Best Website Builders*
https://www.wpbeginner.com/beginners-guide/how-to-choose-
the-best-website-builder/

Article: *Why Your Memoir Won't Sell* by Jane Friedman
https://www.janefriedman.com/memoir-wont-sell/

Article: Wattpad's backstory

https://theliteraryplatform.com/news/2012/10/wattpad-building-the-worlds-biggest-reader-and-writer-community/

St. Martin's unpublished mystery novel contest
https://mysterywriters.org/about-mwa/st-martins/

MONEY MATTERS

CONTRACTS

Alliance of Independent Authors
PDF download (free) *Understanding and Negotiating Book Publishing Contracts*
https://www.authorsalliance.org/wp-content/uploads/2018/10/20181003_AuthorsAllianceGuidePublicationContracts.pdf

Authors Guild
https://authorsguild.org/news/authors-guild-issues-model-trade-book-contract/

Independent Book Publishers Association
A GUIDE TO THE BOOK PUBLISHING AGREEMENT (members only)
https://www.ibpa-online.org/page/fullcontract-members-only

Hybrid Publisher Criteria
https://www.ibpa-online.org/page/hybridpublisher

The Authors Guild *Model Trade Book Contract* (members only)
https://authorsguild.org/resource/model-trade-book-contract/

UNDERSTANDING ROYALTIES

2021 Sisters in Crime Business of Books Survey (Released December 2022)
https://www.sistersincrime.org/page/2021BoBS

ADVERTISING & PROMOTION

Goodreads: https://www.goodreads.com

Author Central: https://author.amazon.com/

BookBub: https://partners.bookbub.com https://insights.bookbub.com

Street Team: https://www.writersdigest.com/publishing-insights/develop-street-team-book

THE WRITE LIFE

ASSOCIATIONS (PARTIAL LIST)

Alliance of Independent Authors: https://www.allianceindependentauthors.org

Canadian Society of Children's Authors, Illustrators and Performers: https://www.canscaip.org

Crime Writers of Canada: https://www.crimewriterscanada.com

Historical Novel Society: https://historicalnovelsociety.org

Independent Book Publishers Association: https://www.ibpa-online.org/default.aspx

Romance Writers of America: https://www.rwa.org

Science Fiction and Fantasy Writers of America: https://www.sfwa.org

Sisters in Crime: https://www.sistersincrime.org/default.aspx

https://www.sistersincrime.org/page/guppy-online-chapter

Society of Children's Book Writers and Illustrators: https://www.scbwi.org/

Writers' Union of Canada: https://www.writersunion.ca

GRANTS

Grant Writing 101 – Jane Friedman
https://www.janefriedman.com/grantwriting-101/

RESOURCES BY CATEGORY

AGGREGATORS, RETAILERS & DISTRIBUTORS

Amazon (Kindle Direct Publishing): https://kdp.amazon.com/en_US/

Apple (iTunes Connect): https://itunespartner.apple.com/books/

Barnes & Noble Nook (B&N Press): https://press.barnesandnoble.com

D2D: https://www.draft2digital.com/Path

Google Play: https://play.google.com/books/publish/u/0/

Kobo (Rakuten Kobo): https://writinglife.kobo.com

Untreed Reads: https://www.untreedreads.com/additionalservices/

AWARDS, CONTESTS & GRANTS

Poets & Writers
https://www.pw.org/grants

St. Martin's unpublished mystery novel contest
https://mysterywriters.org/about-mwa/st-martins/

EDITING & PROOFREADING

Editorial Freelancers Association
https://www.the-efa.org/

Editors Canada
https://www.editors.ca/ode/search

Chartered Institute of Editors and Proofreaders
https://www.ciep.uk/directory/

GOVERNMENT LINKS

Copyright – Treaty Countries
https://www.wipo.int/members/en/

UNITED STATES
https://www.copyright.gov
https://www.copyright.gov/about/fees.html

Register a Business Name
https://www.sba.gov/business-guide/launch-your-business/
register-your-business

Taxes
https://www.irs.gov/businesses/small-businesses-self-employed

CANADA

Copyright Canada
https://www.canada.ca/en/services/business/ip/copyright.html
https://www.ic.gc.ca/eic/site/cipointernet-internetopic.nsf/eng/
wr04196.html

Filing for an HST Number
https://www.canada.ca/en/revenue-agency/services/tax/
businesses/topics/gst-hst-businesses/account-register.html

ISBN Canada
https://www.bac-lac.gc.ca/eng/services/isbn-canada/Pages/
isbn-canada.aspx

Register a Business Name
https://www.canada.ca/en/services/business/start/choosing-a-
business-name-3.html

HELPFUL BLOGS & WEBSITES *some resources not
referenced in text

Career Authors
https://careerauthors.com/

Jane Friedman (reports on book publishing industry)
https://www.janefriedman.com

Kobo – Glossary of Self-Publishing Terms
https://kobowritinglife.zendesk.com/hc/en-us/articles/
360059385491-Glossary-of-Self-Publishing-Terms

NaNoWriMo
https://nanowrimo.org

Ngrams
https://books.google.com/ngrams

QueryLetter.com
https://www.queryletter.com

The Passive Voice
https://www.thepassivevoice.com/contact/

Using Music in your Book
https://www.pdinfo.com/public-domain-music-list.php
http://www.judypenzsheluk.com/2022/01/22/lets-talk-about-writing-using-lyrics/

Writer Beware by Victoria Strauss
https://www.sfwa.org/other-resources/for-authors/writer-beware/

Writers First
https://writers-first.com

PUBLISHERS & PUBLISHING PLATFORMS / INFORMATION

Literary Marketplace
http://www.literarymarketplace.com/

Publishers Marketplace
https://www.publishersmarketplace.com

Query Tracker
https://querytracker.net/

Article: The Odds of Getting Published

https://wordsrated.com/odds-of-getting-published-statistics/

IMPRINTS

Heartdrum: https://www.harpercollins.com/pages/corporate-for-authors-submit-a-manuscript

Yen Press: https://yenpress.com

SELF-PUBLISHING

BOOK REVIEWS

Kirkus Reviews: https://www.kirkusreviews.com/indie-reviews/

Midwest Book Review: https://www.midwestbookreview.com

SOCIAL PUBLISHING

Booksie: https://www.booksie.com/

BookieSilk.com: https://www.booksiesilk.com/

GALATEA (Inkitt sister app) https://getgalatea.com

Inkitt: https://www.inkitt.com/

Kindle Vella: https://www.amazon.com/kindle-vella

Wattpad: https://www.wattpad.com/stories/website

TRADITIONAL PUBLISHERS

Hachette: https://www.hachettebookgroup.com

HarperCollins: https://www.harpercollins.com/

Macmillian Publishers: https://us.macmillan.com

Penguin Random House: https://www.penguinrandomhouse.com/

Simon & Schuster: https://www.simonandschuster.com/

WRITERS' TOOLBOX

DESIGN

Canva
https://www.canva.com

FORMATTING

Adobe
https://www.adobe.com/products/indesign.html

Atticus
https://www.atticus.io

Draft2Digital
https://draft2digital.com/knowledge-base/

Kindlepreneur
https://kindlepreneur.com/how-to-hire-a-book-formatter/

Scrivener
https://www.literatureandlatte.com/scrivener/overview

Vellum

https://store.vellum.pub/

BUILDING A WEBSITE

WPBeginner
www.wpbeginner.com/beginners-guide/how-to-choose-the-best-website-builder/

HOW TO WRITE AN AUTHOR BIO

LiveWriteThrive
https://www.livewritethrive.com/2022/01/31/how-to-write-the-perfect-author-bio

LOGLINES

NFI
https://www.nfi.edu/logline-examples/

AUTHOR'S NOTE

Ten years ago, I made the decision to write a novel. I'd been working as a freelance journalist for a decade, and in addition to contributing to multiple North American consumer and trade publications, I was the Senior Editor of *New England Antiques Journal* and Editor of *Home BUILDER Canada*. I thought my reputation in the industry would help pave the way to publication.

It didn't, and despite my knowledge that publishing was, first and foremost, a business, it also didn't prepare me for the road ahead. Like every naïve author, I too made the requisite number of mistakes along the way. Fortunately, I've been guided by many established authors on my journey, authors who agreed to lend an ear, offer advice, or blurb my books, and I will be forever grateful for their insights and inspiration.

The publishing world can be a cruel one, but it is less so when authors help each other. It is my hope that this book guides you on your own personal journey, and perhaps gives you the push you have been waiting for to finally take your first step.

Dare to dream.

ACKNOWLEDGMENTS

The concept of a book exploring different publishing paths began with a presentation prepared for the New Tecumseth Public Library in early 2022. My thanks to the library, and especially Kim Burgess, the Adult Programming Director, for their ongoing support of local authors and creative content.

The concept was fleshed out further when Alexa Schlosser, Managing Editor of the Independent Book Publishers Association, commissioned an article on presentations for their member's magazine, the *IBPA Independent*, for the May/June 2022 issue. That article took me back to my journalistic routes and led to another connection: K.D. Sullivan, co-founder of Untreed Reads Publishing. K.D. liked the article, recognized my name from a story included in Untreed's *Flash and Bang: A Short Mystery Fiction Society Anthology*, and reached out. Before long, I was telling her about how I thought the presentation might work as a book, and as she helped me to brainstorm ideas, I knew it was something I wanted to pursue.

But wanting to do something and doing it are two different things. One thing I knew for certain was that I couldn't do it alone. Fortunately, fate had brought Emily Nakeff into my life. I'd met Emily a few years before while doing a NaNoWriMo talk at the Essa (Angus) Public Library, and she'd attended other presentations, including *Finding Your Path to Publication* and *Self-publishing: The Ins & Outs of Going Indie*, through the New Tecumseth Public Library. I knew that Emily was an aspiring author, working hard to hone her craft, and that she was also an editor. Hiring Emily to review and edit my weekly output (thereby keeping me accountable to the project) was the best decision I could have made. Her insights, gentle critiques, and suggestions were invaluable to the process and her assistance as a Research Assistant in the creation of the Additional Resources (Talking the Talk, Resources by Section and Category) cannot be overstated.

I also owe a tremendous debt of gratitude to my longtime editor, Ti Locke, for her review and edit of the final manuscript, beta readers Annie McQuaid, Elisabeth McGregor, and K.D. Sullivan, and my proofreader Nicky Hill. Writing a book may be a solitary process, but getting it to the finish line takes teamwork. I could not have come this far without you.

Last, but certainly not least, to the following individuals and organizations who gave permission to quote from their online resources and surveys:

The Alliance of Independent Authors (ALLi)
The Authors Guild
The Book Industry Study Group
The Independent Book Publishers Association
Jane Friedman
Sisters in Crime
WordsRated
WriterBeware

And finally, to the authors, whether aspiring or published and looking for a new path to explore. Thank you for trusting me with your vision.

Judy Penz Sheluk
  May 2023

ABOUT THE AUTHOR

A former journalist and magazine editor, Judy Penz Sheluk is the bestselling author of two mystery series: The Glass Dolphin Mysteries and Marketville Mysteries, both of which have been published in multiple languages. Her short crime fiction appears in several collections, including the Superior Shores Anthologies, which she also edited. With a passion for understanding the ins and outs of all aspects of publishing, Judy is also the founder and owner of Superior Shores Press, which she established in February 2018.

Judy is a member of the Independent Book Publishers Association, Sisters in Crime, International Thriller Writers, the Short Mystery Fiction Society, and Crime Writers of Canada, where she served on the Board of Directors for five years, the final two as Chair. She lives in Northern Ontario. Find her at www.judypenzsheluk.com.